BEXHl

edited by Fred Gray

Falmer
Centre for Continuing Education
University of Sussex
1994

© Centre for Continuing Education, University of Sussex, 1994

ISBN 0 904242 34 X

Front cover designed by Katy Bignell

Published by the Centre for Continuing Education, University of
Sussex, Falmer, Brighton, BN1 9RG
Desktop published using Pagemaker, typeset in Palatino
Printed by Delta Press, 2 Goldstone Street, Hove, BN3 3RJ

CONTENTS

PREFACE

This book contains 14 personal accounts of people who grew up in Bexhill early in the twentieth century. The people whose stories are here were born between 1898 and 1918 and spent all or most of their childhood in Bexhill or nearby. In most cases, too, people stayed on in Bexhill when they left school. If they moved away from the town, they came back later in their lives.

In the autumn of 1988 Fred Gray, the editor of this volume, and Aylwin Guilmant, life long resident of Bexhill and a prolific writer about Bexhill and other places in the south east of England, approached Bexhill Museum with the aiming of starting an oral history project about the town. The Museum's then curator (Stella Bellem) willingly lent support to the idea. An initial large open meeting at the Museum explored the idea, and from this a smaller group formed a workshop - under the auspices of the Centre for Continuing Education at the University of Sussex - to interview some older local people and publish the results as a book. Under the leadership of Aylwin Guilmant and with occasional visits from Fred Gray, the workshop met regularly over the following months until the spring of 1989. Within a year we had gathered a large amount of material, too much, indeed, for one volume. We decided to concentrate on the oldest interviewees, who were born before or during the First World War.

We wanted a cross section of people with different backgrounds and experiences. This meant both men and women from diverse social groups and people from different parts of the area that, during the early part of this century, was rapidly changing from a still largely rural place into a single large urban area centred on the new resort development between the Old Town and the sea front. While keeping to this objective, our choice of whom to approach was guided by very pragmatic considerations, particularly our knowledge of older residents of the town we thought might be willing to be interviewed. In practice many other respondents came from similar backgrounds. For example, some were the sons or daughters of local shop keepers and others had family links with the area around about for two or more generations. As the personal stories recounted in the book show, there were many poor people in Bexhill.

Nonetheless, the picture emerges of a town that was relatively prosperous and comfortable. Bexhill was rather unique. There are relatively few indications of the extremes of poverty found in other Sussex seaside towns such as Hastings and Brighton at the same times, and it did not have the large areas of extremely poor housing true of the older Sussex seaside towns. Indeed, some people living in Hastings looked to Bexhill for work when unemployment and poverty were rife in their own town.

In interviewing people we concentrated on their own experiences as children and young adults and their memories of the area during the period. The interviews were taped. Some lasted for perhaps an hour; in other cases interviewers returned on one or more subsequent occasions because our respondents had so much to say. Our questions varied according to the circumstances. In some cases the people we spoke to needed continual and very specific questions to help them talk about the past; in others our respondents happily recounted their lives with little more than an initial question to set the scene. The result, reflected in this book, is that the interviews varied in content and detail.

Two of the accounts presented here were made in rather different ways. Percy Dowling was interviewed by his son who took shorthand notes during the interview and then typed up the results. Nellie Sinden's account comes from a taped interview made during the mid-1970s. We included this account because we felt it added a further dimension to the interviews gathered by the workshop over a decade later.

An initial stage in processing the information was to transcribe each tape verbatim. From here each transcription was edited into a more readable form telling the story of the individual's life. Where appropriate questions were incorporated into the answers; material covering the same topic but from different stages of each interview was put together into a single section; decisions were made about what to exclude (for example, information about the post war period was mostly left out); and in many cases transcriptions were reordered chronologically. The aim throughout was to make each history into an easily readable account, while trying to maintain its accuracy, essence and 'feel'. The accounts provided here are, therefore, altered 'testimonies', that have been filtered and changed both through the process of interviewing and the editing of each into an accessible story.

Oral history - where people recount their lives and individual histories - provides an antidote to history books prepared using documentary material. It is a valuable means of revealing something of the recent past in particular places and the role of ordinary people in history. Oral history demonstrates that there is no standard history of a particular place or social group, but instead that there are as many histories of a place and time as there are people who experienced them. Although sometimes following well documented trends, in terms of experiences of education, family life, work or housing, for example, peoples detailed experiences vary, sometimes greatly so. Putting together a series of individual histories allows us fresh insights into how people lived, and the changing character of particular places. Talking with people about the past can also provide some vivid insights - in contrast to the often dry bones of standard histories - into what real people did and thought and felt. Readers can have a sense of what it was like to be a child or an adult earlier this century. We can understand, in a personal way, something of what it meant to go to school or be a child in a poor family, or to work as a domestic servant, a fireman, a shop assistant or a bathing hut attendant.

One of the difficulties of talking to people about the past is that of weighing and judging subjective views of their own lives many decades ago. Their own childhoods may have been happy, but those of their parents full of distress. Again, some people contrast a happy childhood with modern ills. One of the challenges posed by oral history is to assess whether such sentiments reflect the personal and individual changes experienced on moving from the relative freedom of childhood to the responsibilities of adulthood, or illustrate a more general change in society over time.

The editing of the accounts and preparation of material in book form was undertaken, over a three year period, by Fred Gray, with an important contribution from Aylwin Guilmant. A first draft of the introduction was written by the late Relf Kenway.

The book represents a team effort of all the people involved in the initial workshop, although some individuals were able to devote much more time to the project than others. The members of the workshop were Margaret Woolf, Jane Kinsella, Richard Chaple, Aylwin Guilmant, Jill Theis, Valerie McPherson, Stella Bellem, Tom

Thomas, Relf Kenway, Jethro Arscott, Peter Vernon, and Anne Vollor. The revised introduction was commented on by Carol Gray, Sara Hinchliffe, Mary Hutchinson and Al Thomson. These people spotted a number of inconsistencies and other inaccuracies that needed to be amended. What errors, factual or otherwise, there are in this book are the responsibility of Fred Gray.

Specific thanks are due to Stella Bellem and Brenda Mason, respectively past and present curators of Bexhill Museum, and the staff of the Museum for various help and assistance, including accommodation when we first met to discuss the project, and the provision of photographs. Bexhill's Old Town Preservation Society allowed us access to the tape of Nellie Sinden being interviewed by Frederick W Hodgson. Most significantly, a great acknowledgement is due to all the people (including those whose stories are not included in this volume) who so willingly agreed to talk with us about their lives as children and young people in Bexhill.

INTRODUCTION

The last great Sussex seaside resort

Present day Bexhill is a town by the sea rather than a seaside resort. By the late twentieth century Bexhill-on-Sea is a substantial and well established town, rather sedate, quiet, and generally prosperous. The pleasant open promenade and sea front road is dominated by Bexhill's most famous building, the architecturally notable De La Warr Pavilion - a 1930s seaside palace of entertainment in Modernist style. Nearby are substantial Edwardian redbrick buildings, often originally designed as hotels, such as the Sackville, but now converted into flats. To the east and west the sea front varies, including both inter-war and post-war detached houses and more recent blocks of flats. Behind the sea front is a mixture of residential streets spanning the period from the late nineteenth century onwards. Heading north and upwards through the present shopping streets and past the Edwardian town hall, many roads eventually lead to

Bexhill Old Town

Bexhill-on-Sea The Fore

Bexhill Old Town, the original settlement, and still a delightful combination of buildings suggesting a small town in rural Sussex in the last century. Within the modern town are other rural vestiges, including the remains of two villages - Little Common and Sidley - still retaining something of their old identity.

Little of today's town suggests that Bexhill was the last great Sussex seaside resort to be built, following a path well trodden in earlier decades by Hastings and Brighton, Bognor and Worthing, and, in the later half of the nineteenth century, by Bexhill's own great rival and nearby neighbour Eastbourne.

In the final decades of the last century and the first decades of this, Bexhill-on-Sea was the boom town of the East Sussex coast. Figures for population change show the situation well. By 1901 12,213 people lived in the town, over five times more than two decades earlier. By 1931 the population had risen to 21,229. The comparison with other Sussex resorts is also revealing. The population of Bexhill increased by 26 per cent and 33 per cent during the two decades from 1901 and 1911. For the 'Empress of Watering Places', Eastbourne, the comparative figures are 21 per cent and one per cent. The population of older Brighton, 'the Queen of Resorts', increased by nine per cent in both decades, while that of Hastings fell by seven per cent in the ten years to 1911 and increased by nine per cent in the following decade. Between 1921 and 1931 Hastings and Eastbourne both lost population (by two and seven per cent respectively), Brighton's population stayed at the same size, while Bexhill, in the midst of national economic decline, still increased by four per cent. In contrast to the other East Sussex resorts (and other places in Britain) Bexhill was a vibrant, growing town for the first 30 years of the century.

Population figures and statistical comparisons do not, however, say anything about how people experienced these changes. Talking with people who lived through the growth of Bexhill can reveal what change meant, literally on the ground, and also uncover the detailed geography, the people and houses, the shops and other businesses, farms and individual fields and footpaths, and even the sounds and smells, of particular parts of Bexhill in the first decades of this century.

Bexhill sea front in the early 1890's - 'an ideal watering-place springing up under the auspices of the Earl De La Warr, the chief landowner'

We used to walk to Bexhill through the fields

The stories recounted here illustrate both the then rural nature of much of what is now Bexhill, and how fields were turned into housing estates and rural lanes into roads. Sidley and Little Common were still villages, separated from the new town - 'From Sidley we used to walk to Bexhill through the fields and join it where the Malet Hall now is.' Even before they were joined to Bexhill as part of a single town, the outlying villages had already started to grow as distinct units with their own character - Little Common as an area favoured by those who wished for a quiet time by the sea, with Sidley attracting new inhabitants from Hastings who wanted a more rural life. Sidley's growth was also aided by the opening of the railway line from Bexhill West to Crowhurst via Sidley in 1902.

Harry Halls also remembers the era before the development of suburban Bexhill: 'I used to go haying, at the side of Collington Woods. You know Collington Avenue; well, between Colebrooke Road and Westville Road there was no houses there. Terminus Avenue wasn't even built. Westville Road - there was only one house and then you went into a field. The next one up before you get

Rural Bexhill - Little Common

to Sutherland Avenue wasn't made [Holmesdale Road]. Cranston Avenue wasn't made; it was only a track. There was two houses on the right going towards Sutherland Avenue, on the corner of Eastwood Road, Downlands Avenue and Downlands Close wasn't made. Out in the middle nearer to Eastwood Road was Offin's, the butchers' slaughterhouse ... You never got houses until you got to Sutherland Avenue ... You went straight across to the other part of Cranston Avenue, and there was a house on the right about 40 yards up, and then a stile and a footpath right across to Collington Lane, to Collington Manor where Daniel Mayer lived. There was a pond. He owned Collington Woods in those days. All that property was his, all through there, Walton Park and all that.'

Looking back on their childhoods and youth many people provide rich descriptions of the gradual transformation of a rural area into a town: 'When you used to leave Sidley station there was a muddy footpath which went down, right down, through to St George's Road where St George's junction is. That was a metalled road from then on. That applied for a good many years. There were buildings, there were houses, but not so many, but they gradually came, and gradually filled in other parts of Bexhill which were all fields. We gradually saw the erosion of lots of open fields. Glenleigh Park was one of our best mushroom fields. It was called the Mill Field in those days, and where the council houses are now, Southlands, that was open parkland, all lovely open parkland, but that was all filled in. Then the era came where they started filling in every little space there was to fill in Bexhill. Its gradually grown and grown and it's almost built up now.'

Feeling right on top of the world

By the turn of the century Bexhill had already been partly transformed into a modern resort. Much of the building in the area south of the railway station had taken place, and only a few isolated plots remained to be built on. Harry Halls, for example, recalls 'vacant plots in Devonshire Road and St Leonard's Road, and front gardens in Western Road.' In 1902 Bexhill Council received its charter. Ebenezer Howard, famous for his crusading work for the creation of new towns combining the best of town and country, became the surprise choice as Bexhill's first mayor. Earl De La Warr, the obvious

Municipal pride - the new town hall circa 1900

choice for this office, was in disgrace and Daniel Mayer - a land-owner, eminent local JP and effectively the deputy mayor - announced he could not afford the time to take part in the affairs of the town.

The combination of a wealthy and active patron, Earl De La Warr, and eager town council, dominated by shop keepers and trades people - making their living by supplying hotels, lodging houses and private schools - did much to shape the nature of Bexhill. Both Earl and councillors had the clear view that they wished to attract prosperous and respectable visitors and residents to the town. This policy patterned everything from the resort facilities to the development of high class residential streets. In the 1890s the seventh Earl De La Warr insisted, for example, on high-class behaviour on that part of the sea front, east of Sea Road, which he controlled, banning various types of entertainers whom he felt encouraged rowdy behaviour. The eighth Earl followed a similar policy of trying to make Bexhill-on-Sea an attractive seaside town for wealthier holiday-makers.

That Bexhill's seaside facilities and entertainments were aimed at the well-off there is no doubt, but the resort also had its go ahead, modern and even risqué attractions, perhaps provided in an attempt to mark it out from staid Eastbourne. It was one of the first resorts to allow mixed bathing from its beaches. At the beginning of the century there was an innovative cycle boulevard on East Parade. More startling still, at Whitsun 1902 the cycle boulevard was used as part of the track for the first motor-races in England. Although at the forefront of modern technology and entertainment, these motor-races provoked an angry reaction from some sea front residents - an early example of the clash between different groups over the character and development of the town, perhaps indicating that even by the turn of the century the seeds had already been sown for Bexhill's transformation into a respectable town by the sea.

Many of our respondents provide valuable insights into seaside Bexhill. We read of the 'enterprising' sand artists who 'used to draw pictures in the sand of cathedrals and other large buildings at low tide'; bathing huts on the beach; fortune tellers (not many when compared with Hastings); the military bands playing at the bandstand at the Colonnade; the Kursaal ('You never came out of there

Bexhill bathing

after two hours without feeling right on top of the world'); the wonderfully descriptive Herr Stanislaus Wurms and his White Viennese orchestra (first engaged as the town's resident band in 1894); Hilda Bor's and Rosie Paikin's Band at the Colonnade; the quintessential respectable seaside resort concert parties; and, the bath chairs ('wicker ones for summer and big black ones with hoods for protection against the weather for use in winter') at the bottom of Sea Road ('ran by a Mr Flea, but he always called himself Flay').

Early on one of the prime places of entertainment was the Kursaal, opened on the sea front in 1896. In 1900 it was leased to JM Glover who was the Director of Music at Drury Lane. Harry Foster talks of how the Kursaal eventually made way for the Pavilion: 'What we also had then was the Kursaal. That was built by Lord De La Warr. It looked like a short pier rather. When I began to know something about it was in the time when it was run by the Pavilion Company and it was managed by Fred Pepper, who was the brother of a more well known Pepper, Harry Pepper. I've been in that place when they've had professional variety shows and not 50 people there. It was getting pretty awful, and then suddenly Philip Yorke and his Barnstormers were invited. They came to the Pavilion, and took off. It put Bexhill right on the map for repertory. Later on Matthew Players used to perform year after year at the De La Warr Pavilion, others too, but that was the sort of repertory in Bexhill.

The Kursaal was a German sounding name and they dropped that during the First World War and it became the Pavilion. By 1935 the Pavilion Company wasn't doing at all well and they wanted to sell it. The Pavilion Company then let off part of the area of the beach, on its west side where the Sailing Club now is, to a firm that made a leisure centre of it. A noisy, brash centre with dodgem cars et cetera, right in the heart of this town. Bexhill couldn't take that and of course they had to buy it. They paid a heavy price for it. Having bought the Kursaal it was pulled down, and so the De La Warr followed on from that.'

The remarkable De La Warr Pavilion was innovative and unique in design, construction and purpose. It was built not only to enter-tain but to simultaneously improve people's 'mental and physical fitness'. The Pavilion, opened in 1935 and commented on by many of our respondents, was the result of an architectural competition insitigated by the town's socialist mayor, the Earl De La Warr.

Buildings for a select resort: The Kursaal and ornamental gates (top) and the Colonnade on its opening in 1911, now the site of the De La Warr Pavilion

The Cycle Boulevard on East Parade, looking towards Galley Hill

Apart from the distinctive seaside attractions, the town had all of the amenities of a prosperous and growing urban area - good rail links, excellent housing, numerous churches and private schools and nursing homes and a wide array of shops. The council was active in providing leisure facilities. There was Egerton Park with its swimming pool, bandstand and sporting amenities. To the west of the park, on the low-lying marshy land between the sea and the railway previously used as a rubbish tip, Polegrove Sports Ground was opened in 1923. By 1925 there were three golf-courses - Galley Hill, Cooden Beach and Highwoods. Visitors and local people alike could enjoy a vast range of sports, becoming members of various sporting clubs including those for cricket, football, roller-skating, rowing and sailing. For the more sedentary cinemas, too, were an attraction. The Bijou in Town Hall Square was opened in 1910 and in 1929 people were able to watch the first talking pictures. The Playhouse was the second cinema to open, in 1921 and it still operates today as the Curzon. The Ritz and the Gaiety cinemas were opened in the 1930s.

Bexhill had additional attractions marking it out from the run of the mill. It was new and modern, middle-class and respectable. It had the advantages of a seaside location surrounded by a rural hinterland. It was far from the squalor and decay, crime and poverty, of the older big cities; problems partly shared by established seaside towns such as Brighton and Hastings.

A very divided place

Being a respectable seaside town was the life blood, the essence, of Bexhill. The town wasn't simply a resort where visitors spent a short period of time. Instead, Bexhill quickly became a residential town by the sea, where people with independent means came to live. All this had major consequences for the geography of the town and the work opportunities available to most people. Evelyn Older describes the situation well: 'Bexhill was a very divided place. Three-quarters worked as servants, gardeners, boot boys ... Dorset Road, Cantelupe Road. All those houses were occupied by one family with not less than three servants. That side - that's where all the work was. Then the shops had a little van and a man who went out to get orders and an errand boy, so everybody was employed as staff of the shops and all the people in those big houses were waited on hand and foot. Even half a pound of butter used to be taken out to Cooden. It was quite a journey to get to Cooden. In Amherst Road they were all private houses. Big houses employed all the people. There were lots of schools; Manor Road had the Beehive, with a lot in Hastings Road.'

More than most English seaside resorts, Bexhill was a town of the British empire. The private schools provided safe if sometimes strict havens for children while their parents were abroad serving the empire, and in Reg Cane's view 'Bexhill was all schools before the last war.' Many former colonial servants saw Bexhill as a natural retirement town. Over time this had its impact on the shape and character of the town. A number of Bexhill's mayors had previously worked overseas: 'Indian army retired' as Reg Cane describes it. We also hear from Harry Foster, who worked for an estate agent between the wars, of how Bexhill as a seaside resort influenced the nature of the property market in the town including the renting of furnished houses to 'people home from abroad for long vacations', letting beach huts, 'people coming here in retirement and buying houses', and 'people who bought houses to run as apartments or guest houses such as Albany Road, Albert Road and Wilton Road.'

What of the areas where the working class of Bexhill lived? Away from the town proper, villages retained their distinctive character-istics and were more socially mixed. As Bert Kiff says of Sidley: 'Generally speaking as far as Sidley was concerned we knew every-body and everybody knew us. But now we know nobody. It's different. One of the differences of course in the Sidley area they were all rented houses, and now they are nearly all self owned.'

Nellie Sinden's story, amongst others, shows there was also considerable neighbourhood and community self-help and support in the working class areas of Bexhill: 'everybody helped one another in those days, everybody was very friendly, everybody knew one another simply because it was a small community. If your parents were not well, the next door neighbour would come in.' But occa-sionally the accounts hint at another more violent side of family and neighbourhood life: 'There was a lot of drinking in the town. Some

Sea Road, 1911, showing on the right the gates marking the entrance to the De La Warr parade

of the husbands were quite rough. Very rough.'

For many working class families space was at a premium; there were sometimes several children sharing a bedroom. And to make ends meet families might take in lodgers. Percy Dowling's mother 'always had lodgers. Of course, in the summer she had holiday people staying. We had one family who used to come for two weeks every year. It was hard work. Very often, my mother would have two families - one in the front room, and one in the rear room, and the two bedrooms front and rear upstairs.' Families also often moved house as family fortunes changed. Mr Dowling's parents 'got the wanderlust. We started at 53 Cornwall Road and finished up in 26. The joke was, before we left 53, my mother and father were offered the house for £150 and they could not even afford that in those days. The houses in Cornwall Road were biggish, two rooms downstairs, and a kitchen and scullery; three up and then you had the attic - but of course, you never had a bathroom.' Most people rented from private landlords. There was little council housing, and home ownership was the exception, especially for working class families.

Life was difficult

For many working class parents feeding and clothing children, paying the rent, and making ends meet on a day to day basis was an enduring problem. Harry Foster, the son of a cobbler in Windsor Road tells how: 'My brother worked in my father's business and we were extremely poor, notwithstanding the fact that none of us drank, smoked or gambled. My father had a 10 rod allotment in Terminus Road - it was very, very heavy clay soil and very hard work keeping it going - and my mother did charing and occasionally let a room to balance the books.' Allotments were a crucial way for families to provide enough to eat, and for some children helping dad on the allotment was - sometimes to their dismay - a normal part of the week. 'Every family had their own allotments. They grew all their veg on it: enough potatoes to store for the winter to help through til potatoes came again.'

Again, as Olive Wright says 'Life was very hard for my mother. She had 11 children; two of them died.' In larger, poor families children had brothers and sisters to look after or be looked after by, and clothes and toys were re-used: 'the older ones, where there was

21

a big family, really were the drudge to the family because the older ones were expected to help mother all she or he possibly could.' Running a house and family and making ends meet was also time consuming, and some of our respondents talk of the daily and weekly routine followed by their mothers.

The people we interviewed were children just as the foundations were being laid of what was to become known as the welfare state. For the parents of some of our respondents it was too little or too late. Health care, for example, was still a largely private matter, and a variety of stories are told about how people responded to sickness and ill-health. In some cases women took on the role of neighbourhood midwife and someone to call on in times of sickness: 'She went round helping with all these things ... she'd sit up during the night and get the kids' breakfast the next morning.' Sometimes people paid a regular weekly amount to join a doctor's panel, or joined a friendly society (such as 'the Tunbridge Wells Equitable Friendly Society') to guard against the unforeseen.

Very frequently families were broken up, most often by the death of the male breadwinner. Some of the oldest of our respondents remember the time before widows' pensions provided by the state were introduced. Reg Cane tells how his father, a horse van driver, died of consumption: 'My poor mum was left with the three of us. No widow's pensions, no nothing those days.' Widowed parents suddenly thrown into extreme poverty were forced to take whatever work was available - 'charing or scrubbing' in the private schools, or dressmaking at home, while still looking after home and children. Although the introduction of widows pensions undoubtedly helped, women left alone with their children were still hard up. Bert Kiff's mother, widowed when her husband was killed at sea during the Great War, 'found work in the orchards to help supplement her pension.' For Nellie Sinden the death of her father 'meant my mother having to go out to work again. She went on at midwifery or helped with an undertaker to do the last offices. As the children got older, naturally they were glad for them to go out and earn what they could to help bring in the money.' Many working class children had to contribute to the family income as soon as possible, sometimes before they left school. Often, though, extended families also helped out. We hear how aunts and uncles or grandparents, often sharing the family home, were sometimes centrally involved in bringing up children and, for some people, helping to run the family business.

The collection of accounts in this book undermines some of the often repeated generalisations about the large families supposedly commonplace in the past. One of our respondents had eight brothers and sisters (and two more who died at birth). Two others had four siblings each. But most of the people whose stories are recounted here were only children or had just one or two brothers or sisters. By the early decades of this century in a town like Bexhill small families seem to have been quite usual. In talking with people we never probed deeply about the more personal dimensions of family life. For example, there is little or no mention of sex. But while some women clearly had little choice in the matter (their husbands dying when they were still young, or because of ill health) others, presumably, decided voluntarily to limit the size of their families.

A real do for everybody

Despite the poverty of many families, most of our respondents also recount the pleasures of being children and young adults. Many have fond memories of playing with their parents or childhood friends, and of adventures around the town or exploring the surrounding countryside. We read of 'Tibby cat' and iron hoops made by blacksmiths. There were many temptations for children and being caught doing something wrong often met with swift physical retribution from parents, teachers, police or other adults: 'If a policemen caught you doing a silly thing he would just clip you 'side the ear. If he was carrying his cape on his shoulder, he would fling the cape round the back of your head and give you one.'

There are also accounts of celebrations of family and annual holidays and celebration. Christmas, for example, was 'a real do for everybody.' Food is sometimes lovingly remembered: 'We always had enough to eat. It was Sussex pudding, suet pudding, vegetables and gravy. We had our own little allotment. Puddings were usually jam roly polys and that sort of thing, cause it was the war years and food was short.'

The influx of troops into the area during the Great War also left a lasting impression on a number of people. Some local boys struck up friendships with troops in the area. For Reg Cane going to the Cooden camp was his chance to watch boxing matches between the soldiers stationed there and play football in a local team against the Service Invalids. Alice Eldridge, talking about the fun of meeting Canadian and American troops based in the area, says there was 'no trouble with any of them. Sex never was mentioned.' Our respondents say little (and were asked little) about sex, although for both young men and women finding a sweetheart was a significant and memorable event.

One of the most remarked upon features of leisure for many young people was Bexhill's Athletic Club. A number of people talk about the history of the club, the delights of many open air activities (especially camping and swimming in the Highwoods) and the major impact it had on their lives. Reg Cane, for over 40 years the leader of the Athletic Club and then its President, describes the early years of the Club in the archway stable loft above a haulage firm ('with the cobwebs and candle grease'), then Malet Hall, and the move in 1922 to Hamilton's garage at the back of the fire station in Amherst Road.

From other people we hear about a host of organisations and facilities, many linked to churches or fostered by the town council, catering for children and young people: 'the Children's Special Service Mission on the beach'; Brownies and Girl Guides; prayer meetings and bible readings; tennis courts and the swimming baths at Egerton park (surprisingly, perhaps, a fair number of our respondents did not like swimming in the sea); boys' clubs; football and cricket teams; the Artisan Section of the Bexhill Golf Club; the Bexhill Angling Club; the Red Cross; choirs and the Bexhill Chorus; the four cinemas in the town by the end of the 1930s; and, of course, the many other seaside attractions to be enjoyed as local residents.

A number of our respondents suggest 'no one ever went away' for a holiday away from home, and Sunday school outings and other organised day trips were notable events in the lives of many children. Queenie Jewhurst describes how 'we used to go on Sunday school treats, because my father was one of the leading lights at the church. We used to go to Pevensey Bay and Norman's Bay by train and be down at the beach all the time. We used to wear these great paddling drawers, like navy blue school bloomers, horrible huge things.'

Middle class families, in contrast, might spend part of the summer holidays away from Bexhill. Paul Allan Hodgkinson mentions his family let their own house in Clifford Road and rented rooms or a house in Tunbridge Wells for the summer holidays. 'It was very convenient for father because he could come down to Bexhill to see about his business.' For a child in a middle class family the pattern of formal and informal leisure was often quite different. We read of nurseries and maids; horse riding, private tennis courts and croquet; and dancing and music lessons: 'We were taught to play the piano by a German teacher. She was Frau Von Hippius and she was quite a socialite ... I think she was well born in Germany.'

Friday morning we used to have a bit of religion

In Bexhill, as most other towns, the two sets of institutions with a major influence on most people's childhoods were church and school. Both were closely intertwined, with the church still having a major role in education. Local schools were, for example, named after the parish they were in. Throughout England central and local government became increasingly involved in schooling. Following the 1902 Education Act, which abolished the chaotic School Board system, the newly created Bexhill Town Council formed an education committee responsible for all board and voluntary schools in the borough. By then the Old Town was served by St Peter's Schools. The girls' and the infants' schools in Barrack Road were built in 1862. St Peter's Boys school, opened in 1853, was in Holliers Hill. There had been a school in Little Common since 1855 and another in All Saints Lane, Sidley, opened in 1865. As seaside Bexhill grew south of the railway line so schools were established for children in the new parish of St Barnabas. The infants' school was opened in 1893 and the St Barnabas' Boys School in Reginald Road five years later. With the continued growth of Bexhill the Downs School (now King Offa and Bexhill High Schools) was built in two stages, in 1907 and 1912.

Many of our respondents describe what going to school in Bexhill was like in the early part of this century. We hear, for instance, about the layout of schools and classrooms, what was taught, sports and playground games, the personalities of teachers and fellow pupils, clothing, school ceremonies and traditions, and discipline. Percy Dowling illustrates some of these topics: 'I went to St Barnabas' School, which was in Reginald Road. "Caley" Poulton was the headmaster. He was a big churchman. He was a very good man as

Class II St Barnabas Boys School, undated

a teacher, very good. He was greatly respected, all the old boys used to come back, you know - sailors and soldiers and all that sort of thing. They all came to see Caley. You got the cane if you misbehaved. He was quite strict. But Mitchell, the man directly under Caley, he was a villain. He would hold your cheek - like that - and smack your side of the ear with the other hand! He was a vicious bloke.' Harry Halls went to the same school, and recalls that on 'Friday morning we used to have a bit of religion. The Reverend Mortlock used to come from St Barnabas to take prayers about half to three quarters of an hour, with no teeth in!'

Nellie Sinden talks of the role of schools in Empire Day celebrations. 'Each class walked behind our teacher, two-by-two, to Egerton Park. All the schools done the same thing and we all met in Egerton Park round the flag-pole. There was a parson there who gave a very short sermon. We had a hymn and a prayer and then we all sang "Land of our birth we pledge to thee". We all walked round the flag, saluted at a certain spot, went back to school and dispersed.'

The 1902 Act also introduced a system of secondary schools and free grammar school education. New county grammar schools were built, with some places reserved for pupils who passed the 'scholarship' examination entitling them to free secondary education. There was no secondary school in Bexhill and scholarship children had to travel to Lewes. Ivy Fuller tells of the journey walking and by train from Sidley to Lewes. This remained the case until the Bexhill boys' and girls' County Secondary (subsequently Grammar) Schools were built in 1925-26. Evelyn Older comments on the new schools: 'If you were clever at school they had to pass an examination to go to what was the secondary school in Turkey Road, now the College. Only a very few passed. If they passed they were allowed some money for their books and things.' Distinctions emerged between scholarship pupils, marked out for better things, and the educationally less successful, most of whom left school and started work at the earliest opportunity.

As we have seen, however, Bexhill's education system was rather unique. Apart from the state system of schooling, catering for local, working class children and duplicated in towns and cities throughout England, there was also a distinct and separate, large and influential, private school sector. At their peak there were more than 30 private 'independent' schools in the town, aimed in only a marginal way at local children. Instead they were part and parcel of Bexhill-on-Sea as a respectable resort: 'The town was full of private schools and laundries and it was that which kept Bexhill going.' Many took in boarders, children whose parents were often abroad, perhaps in the armed forces or administrative services of the Crown serving the widespread British empire. Such parents visited their children in Bexhill on leave, and many eventually retired to the town. Hastings Road was the first area of the town to become dominated by private schools, although after the turn of the century others were opened in the Collington area with the co-operation of the trustees of the Ebenezer Howard estate (Bexhill's first mayor).

Although our respondents are aware of the importance of private schools in the town, few experienced them as pupils. They were, instead, more likely to provide direct or indirect job opportunities such as charring, delivering, beating carpets, and making dresses. Nonetheless, better off local families did send their children to one or two private schools in the town or further afield. For Queenie Jewhurst 'My first school was Mountcroft in Parkhurst Road. I think most of the town's business people's children went there.' She subsequently continued her private education at Wellington College in Wellington Square, Hastings.

Private schools provided opportunities not available in the state sector, both in terms of what was taught and extra-curricular activities such as music and dancing. Children at private schools were marked out, too, by their uniforms: 'Uniforms at Mountcroft was just green and white bands round our straw hats and a badge, on our pockets of our blazers and green Tam o' Shanters in the winter. But Wellington was black, black bands round our Panamas and a metal badge, gold and orange. And we had to wear grey and yellow blouses under our gym tunics. It was a horrible colour.'

Whether a Bexhill child attended a state or private school was clearly an important divide. Nellie Sinden ends her account of the Empire Day celebrations by saying: 'The private schools didn't go down to Egerton Park naturally. Just the elementary schools.' Some of our respondents suggest there was little out-of-school mixing between local children going to different types of school. This seems likely because of the contrasts in social and family backgrounds, and the way the poor and rich in Bexhill, as most other towns, lived in distinct areas. But other people indicate their friends as children and young adults were drawn from a wide range of backgrounds. And while state and private schools divided local children, they might be thrown together in other ways, particularly when going to church and taking part in church social activities (although some churches catered for distinct social groups and excluded others).

Well into this century the church appears to have continued to play a central role in the everyday life of many people in Bexhill. It was normal for children to go to church or Sunday School three times each Sunday. Apart from faith and religion and the services that structured the Sabbath, the churches provided Sunday School treats and outings and various religious and social activities for children and adults during the week. When Nellie Sinden was 17 and in service, 'When I got home (in the evenings) I used to go to the Girl Guides or Rangers, used to help with the Brownie Pack, or Prayer Meeting on a Monday evening, Bible reading on a Thursday evening. I didn't take up dancing til later years.'

Some families were flexible in their choice of places to worship: 'We were not a very strict religious family, though we went to church regularly on Sunday. We started off where Father was a

Building St Barnabas Church

sideman at St Peter's, we were all baptised there. When Father thought things were rather high church there we went to St Stephen's on the Down ... Occasionally Father took us to St Barnabas for Evensong. I sometimes went to the Presbyterian church where my Mother went. I was in the choir there.'

By the inter-war years the town had a full range of places of worship meeting the needs of residents and visitors alike. The Old Town had the ancient parish church of St Peter's. St Mark's in Little Common was built in 1842. The parish of St Barnabas covering the new town was created in 1891. St Stephen's church was consecrated in June 1900. At the turn of the century Anglican Church services in Sidley were held in the Iron Church; the first services held in the permanent All Saints Church were on All Saints Day 1910. A Roman Catholic mission opened in July 1893 on the site of the present church of St Mary Magdalene. For Methodists there was the older Belle Hill Mission and by 1900 churches in Sackville Road, Little Common and Sidley. Beulah Baptist Church opened in 1898 and in the second decade of this century the Baptists erected an iron church, always known as Haddon Hall, on land in Sidley Street. The Congregational Church in Station Road (now London Road) was opened in the same month as Queen Victoria's Diamond Jubilee. One of the two foundation stones of St George's Presbyterian Church of England in Cantelupe Road was laid by Countess De La Warr on Easter Monday 1901.

The Salvation Army Hall was opened in 1914 although many services continued to be held in the open air on the Down or in Town Hall Square. Harry Foster's parents were Salvationists, and his account demonstrates the importance of the Army in their life, particularly on Sundays: 'My parents were both members of the local Salvation Army Corps. My father was in the band, was band-master at one stage; my brother also was in the band. My mother sang. On Sunday, it meant that about 10 o'clock, or soon after, they would join what they called an open air meeting in one or two roads of the town until 11 o'clock when they would go to their Citadel or Hall. It used to be in a top room in Windsor Road, but later on it was in London Road where it still is. In the afternoon they would go to another open air meeting which, in the summer, would be on the West Beach, near the Clock Tower. And then in the evening they had an early service, sometimes outside, and then to the hall again. So one can say that, apart from meals, the whole of their Sunday was occupied by their attendance at the Salvation Army outside or inside.'

You couldn't better yourself in any possible way

Working class school children frequently took on various jobs outside school hours, sometimes bringing in money to supplement the family income and on other occasions helping in the family business. As Reg Cane says: 'Life was difficult. I must have started work when I was about 11 ... I was doing three different jobs before I left school. I done a paper round for Jillo (the) newsagent; ... then this cobblers round in the evening (collecting and taking back school shoe repairs); and each Saturday I worked all day for Pratley ... taking out greengroceries.' Daisy Spandley tells how even as a young child she worked on her adopted parents' nursery: 'I went to school and thought this was lovely - no work to do, but when I got home it was all saved for me. In the garden, feed the chicken, pick fruit according to season, pricking out, watering ... whatever job there was to be done.'

Seaside Bexhill provided other job opportunities for young people: 'In the school holidays I worked for the Bexhill Bathing Company. It was right opposite the putting course. They were the first bathing huts ever to have a shower. I used to take the tickets at the huts, wash towels, we had a wooden thing there, with a scrubbing board and a wringer. I remember, it used to be Hudson's Soap we used, in packets ... I was in the hut from which we sold the tickets, chocolate, minerals and all sorts of things. A couple came off the ramp from the bathing huts, to go up the steps to the sea front, when the woman's knickers dropped off! So with presence of mind, I said to the lady "Step in here", which she did. I shut the cabin door. She had snatched up her knickers and was able to go in, and put them on. She gave me half a crown and they went off. Half a crown was worth having!'

Many children were, then, already used to working before they left school, and it was normal for the sons and daughters of working class parents to leave school at the earliest opportunity, perhaps taking the 'labour exam' at 14 or 15. However much children enjoyed school, the need for them to become full time breadwinners and contribute to the family income was great.

The Sackville, the Devonshire, Channel View, San Remo, the Hotel Riposa. The names of the hotels and houses in Bexhill-on-Sea echo with the resonance of the middle class English seaside early this

31

The beach - pleasure for most, work for others

century. Given the times and the place it is no surprise, then, that most working class girls in Bexhill had a limited range of job opportunities: 'After leaving school girls went in a shop. And if there wasn't enough room in a shop it was more or less domestic service and that's all there was.' The same point is made by another respondent: 'There were no opportunities for other kinds of work. Nothing at all, not when we were young, it was shops or service, and for the lads errand boy.' As a prosperous seaside town there were hotels, guest houses and apartment buildings, independent schools, nursing and convalescent homes, and private houses all using great numbers of female servants of one sort or another.

Being in service was often exhausting drudgery. There was little or no freedom. Hours were long, 12 or more each day. Domestic servants 'living in' had perhaps one afternoon a week and every other Sunday off. Much of the often pitiful pay was either retained by the employer on one pretence or another or sent home to help supplement the family income. Nellie Sinden provides a graphic and detailed description of the worst of being in service. As she points out, once in service there was little chance of ever doing anything else - 'One couldn't rebel, there was nowhere else to go ... You couldn't better yourself in any possible way.' Evelyn Older confirms this view and adds: 'They didn't treat you as a person.' However, she looks back on her final job in service more positively: 'The last people I cooked for used to cater for families there. It was a lovely job.' But by the end of the inter-war years domestic service was in crisis and beginning to fade from its dominant position as a source of work. This general decline as experienced by individuals in various ways: 'At the end I'd risen to the height of housekeeper. Then I did the cooking and looking after them - eight people. There were only four servants at the end, until they gradually dwindled.'

For many women the one escape route was through marriage and starting a family. But national and international events had some impact on women's work in Bexhill. The best illustration is provided by Evelyn Older, who at the beginning of the Second World War left her job as a cook and went to the Morris House garage at the south end of Sackville Road to make aircraft parts for the war effort: 'I had

The Sackville with newly laid out garden

Bandstand and Marine Mansions

to do it, I was re-directed ... Mind you, I enjoyed it. It was so interesting, I was turning a lathe.'

The other limited job opportunities available to most women included working in a shop or laundry, charing or making clothes (work many married and widowed women did part time as a vital contribution to the family income). Our respondents make little mention of clerical work such as typing, only just becoming established as a major job opportunity for women. It still retained considerable mystique and involved a changing new technology. Harry Foster, for example, describes the office processes in a firm of estate agents, and the firm's 'most efficient typist and interviewer, highly efficient', who was the daughter of the Battle Abbey Agent. For the daughters of middle class families there was a broader although still limited range of work, such as teaching, in the expanding professions. Later in life single women left money by their parents might buy a shop or become the proprietor of an hotel or guest house.

Many of our respondents, both male and female, worked in shops on leaving school. It was quite normal for men to be assistants in, for example, grocery shops that are nowadays dominated by women workers. But there were differences between people employed as errand boys or shop assistants, those whose parents rented a small grocery and provisions store selling 'practically everything, from a pin to an elephant', and people whose parents were relatively well off, owning substantial businesses. The Bexhill business community was close knit. Amid competition and rivalry, shopkeepers helped each other out in times of need. For example, we learn of one baker making bread for his rival after a fire and a corner shopkeeper helping out another who had fallen ill. The sons and daughters of prosperous middle class shopkeepers and trades people left school later, and boys might be apprenticed with a firm elsewhere to learn the family business. Paul Allan Hodgkinson was an apprentice for three years at Weekes in Tunbridge Wells. Harry Foster seems to have been relatively exceptional in not following in the footsteps of his father who had a small shoe repair business, but instead started work as an office boy and general dogsbody with an estate agent, eventually working his way to much better jobs in the same firm.

Harry Halls provides a rich account of his mother's grocery and provisions shop in Windsor Road: 'We sold milk and paraffin, the paraffin was out the back. Everything came in bulk. Sugar was all in

Western Road circa 1900

Hessian sacks, two hundredweight. Common washing soda was in Hessian sacks, and everything had to be weighed up in those days. Children used to come in with a basin for a pennyworth of jam, a pennyworth of syrup, a pennyworth of treacle. The vinegar used to be in barrels; Sarson's vinegar wasn't in bottles. Look at bananas, for instance - the price of them now - they go by the pound. In my young day, they went threepence a 'hand' a big bunch of bananas, more than five. Look at swedes; we sold bushels of swedes - a penny each - and now they go by the pound.'

Shop workers had a long working day, particularly on Saturdays: 'People never got paid until after six o'clock Saturday night. My mother used to open her shop half past seven Saturday morning and she wouldn't close till one o'clock Sunday morning.' Hours of work in hotels were sometimes worse - Percy Dowling talks of working from 6.30 in the morning until ten at night with two hours off for dinner, but the tips were often very good: 'I remember my first Christmas there. I made £25 in Christmas tips, and that was a lot of money in those days.'

As an expanding town the building industry was active and for much of the period the largest source of work for men. Some of our male respondents started work in shops or hotels but then moved into the building trades, to be plasterers and plumbers, for example: 'when I was 16 and a half, I went into plumbing. I had had enough of grocery and being indoors and that.' Being an apprentice in one of the building trades held out the promise (sometimes unfulfilled) of better work and wages in the future, but learning the trade was hard and low paid.

Bexhill was a service town and lacked large scale industry unlike Brighton, for example, which had its railway works and a host of associated industrial concerns. One of our respondents suggests that after the First War 'for men folk there wasn't much work in Bexhill. Building might have just been starting and those that were lucky to get jobs in Bexhill got them and those that didn't had to go to Battle or Hastings. They had to walk. Bicycles were very, very few and naturally they hadn't the money to afford to buy a bicycle.' Men coped with unemployment in a number of ways, often taking on essentially casual work. Some returning troops became barrow boys. On other occasions men looked to work from the schools, houses and hotels in the town: 'When they wanted to earn extra money men used to go round to the schools and the hotels and the private houses with their handcarts, collect the carpets and roll them up, take them down on to the Downs in Little Common Road and beat away ...'

Despite the relative prosperity of the resort, Bexhill was not completely immune to many of the economic changes sweeping through Britain between the wars. Harry Foster, for example, argues that: 'the General Strike had no great impact on a place like Bexhill such as it would in a city. The General Strike was only a week, so it didn't affect rent collecting.' But after the Strike estate agency business 'continued to be pretty awful. I can remember having as many as 300 places on the books at times ... There must have been weeks when we didn't sell anything.' Although Bexhill escaped the worst excesses of economic recession, the expansion of the town slowed with consequences for the building industry and building workers: 'When the Labour Exchange was in London Road I saw queues of men down there. They were local people who were unemployed and the unemployment situation was bad because building had quietened down.' Harry Halls, a plumber, was forced to move to London to work on a new LCC housing estate.

A few occupations for men were relatively secure and provided a job for life. Tom Pratt, for instance, discusses in fascinating detail working in the town's fire service. Mr Pratt, who started work when he was 14 as a messenger boy with the Bexhill Fire Brigade, talks of the camaraderie and pride of fire fighters.

Really everybody walked everywhere

At the turn of the century the railways had a dominant position in long distance travel, and were of crucial importance in the development of seaside resorts from the mid-nineteenth century to the 1930s. For Bexhill the railway was an invaluable link with other parts of the country, speedily bringing people and goods to the town. The building of the railway embankment along the coast also acted as a necessary sea defence allowing the development of land to the north of the railway. Bexhill proper was served by two major stations - the Central Station on the coast line and West Station on the later Crowhurst branch line. Although during the first half of the century road transport by tram, coach or bus steadily became more significant, the railways fed into most dimensions of life in Bexhill. Reg

The West Station, circa 1920

Cane, as a schoolboy working for a newsagent, tells of being up 'extra early' to collect newspapers from the station: 'These papers always come in on the Crowhurst line at West Station and we had to push this great wicker basket like postmen had for parcels with a big wheel we had to get them back to the shop for sorting, before the lads come in. I went straight to school from the shop - fainted a time or two - you're running all the way.'

But for most people during the first two decades of the century, moving around Bexhill or to Hastings or the villages around about meant walking, cycling or using the horse. Especially for poorer people, getting from one place to another meant walking. They simply could not afford anything else. Some people walked daily to and from Hastings for work. Families might walk many miles to visit relatives on Sundays or at Christmas time and young women in domestic service in Bexhill often walked 'home' to a rural village once a week. 'Really everybody walked everywhere. If you went to see relations at Ninfield or Hooe or Ashburnham or wherever it was, well you just went on your own two feet. If there were two or three kiddies they were bundled in the pram.'

Especially up until the First War, the horse, though, was king as far as transport within Bexhill was concerned. 'You could tell each horse. They had a certain patter of their hooves going up and down.

There was King, there was Butler ... you couldn't mistake them going up and down with a different patter.' In remembering their childhoods many of our respondents talk about the sights, sounds and smells of the blacksmiths in the town, the importance of horse transport of delivering goods around Bexhill, their various childhood adventures around horses, and the disastrous impact on haulage firms when horses were requisitioned for the war effort. Percy Dowling gives one illustration of childhood play around horses: 'In the old cab days you would sit on the axle. There was plenty of room but if someone yelled "Whip behind!" the old cabby would flick the whip over, and give you one round the face. Well they didn't travel very fast, you could sit on and have a ride.'

New technology, motorised transport and road building eventually helped relegate old forms of transport and contributed to the development of a large and modern new town. The significance of these changes are illustrated by Fred Gillham, a childhood resident

Bexhill horse parade 1914

Public transport at the junction of Sea Road, Station Road and Magdalen Road, 1920's

of Little Common (whose story is not included in this book): 'In my school days Little Common was a community on its own. If one walked from Little Common to Bexhill there was nothing but fields between with just an odd house here and there. If one wanted a doctor, if one had no horse you walked from Little Common to Bexhill Old Town to find a doctor. If you were too ill then the doctor would come out on horse-back. Little Common was a typical country village with its wheelwright shop with a pond beside it where the horses used to be put in while the carts were being repaired and directly opposite was the blacksmith's shop where the wheelwright used to take the wheel after he finished making it and have the iron rim fitted. The horses were taken across there for shoeing ... The changes came when the roads were widened, especially Barnhorn Road, and then Little Common was no longer a village.'

Several existing roads were unsuitable for motor traffic and were widened; in other cases new ones were built, such as the De La Warr, Barnhorn, and London roads. Our respondents also talk about other forms of public transport which encouraged the development of the town, making travelling between different neighbourhoods much easier. The first omnibus service in the town had been started in 1901 and some of our contributors mention the bus which ran from Sidley to Bexhill. A tram service, partly across fields, started in 1906 between Hastings and Cooden and in 1928 the trams were replaced by trolley buses. By the Second World War the motor car had effectively replaced the horse and the street had become a far more dangerous place for children's play.

When war was declared the band was playing

Wider national and international events were felt in various ways by local people. The Great War in particular left lasting memories. Percy Dowling remembers a personal watershed between the Edwardian summer and a world at war: 'The town was very busy in summer. We always had a military band which used to play at the bandstand at the Colonnade before the war. We lads used to sit on that piece facing the sea you know, because it was always crowded, hundreds of people. I remember in 1914 when war was declared the band was playing. When they got the news they immediately packed up and went out of the town.' Harry Foster, in contrast, has a vivid recollection of being told of the armistice that ended the Great War on 11th November 1918.

The impact of the First World War was considerable. Fathers and

Peace Day, 1919

PEACE DAY, BEXHILL-ON-SEA   JULY 19 1919.
VIELER, PHOTO, BEXHILL.

sweethearts were killed, with major consequences for the lives of some of our respondents. Bert Kiff was three years old when his father was killed on 'New Year's Day 1915, when HMS Formidable was lost.' Alice Eldridge recounts how when working as a domestic servant in an apartment house in Cantelupe Road two German waiters - 'they were spies, and none of us knew' - upped and left on the outbreak of the Great War. She also tells how her own sweetheart was killed in the war. And yet the same war 'was marvellous' as an opportunity to meet and mix with overseas troops stationed in Bexhill. When she was only 15 Olive Wright met her husband to be when he was stationed in Bexhill during the First War. Almost immediately after the first brief encounter he was sent to France and badly gassed. When eventually reunited they both went to India.

Reg Cane tells of his indelible childhood memory of the early days of the First World War, passing a private school housing refugees from Belgium and troops feeding 'all their bits and pieces to the Belgian refugees who used to line the railings of the playground.' The school itself had previously been run for German boys by Blasnik, a German, who was interned at the outbreak of the war and the school requisitioned. From other people we hear about rationing and queuing for food, a German Zeppelin airship 'coming out of England and out across the Channel. It was so low you could see the blokes standing there', and the rumble of guns from France. But in comparison with the Second War the town 'was quite ordinary. You would go about in the ordinary way, there were no air raids or things like that.'

June 1940 saw the end of another era for Bexhill. With the fall of France the town, in common with the rest of the English Channel coast became Britain's front line. German invasion was expected at any time. Many inhabitants left the town for safer areas of the country; several of the private schools moved away, never to return. Compared with other towns in Britain, Bexhill suffered very little structural damage in the Second World War. Few of the buildings were destroyed, but the town was damaged in more nebulous ways. After the Second War Bexhill-on-Sea never recaptured its earlier role as a premier holiday resort.

A note on money

Our respondents talk of rent, wages and the cost of everyday necessities using old money, the pre-decimal system of pounds, shillings and pence. There were 12 pence in a shilling and 20 shillings in a pound (and so one pound was worth 240 pence). A florin was two shillings, half a crown two shillings and six pence, and a crown five shillings. One shilling was also known as a bob, while a guinea was 21 shillings. Half pennies and farthings (half and a quarter of a penny respectively) were also in circulation. To convert old into new money divide old pennies by 2.4. One old penny equals less than half a new pence (NP), .467 to be precise; sixpence became 2.5 NP; a shilling five NP; half a crown 12.5 NP; a guinea one pound and five NP; and so on. So 15 shillings and eight pence is nowadays equal to just over 78 NP. The only consistent feature between old money and the decimal system is that a pound remained a pound, although compared with today in the times our respondents talk about ten shillings and one pound came in bank notes - not in 50p and £1 coins.

Readers should also bear in mind that in some cases at least quoted prices and costs should be interpreted with caution. On such matters memory may play tricks over a period of more than a half a century. Inflation also makes comparisons with the present day difficult, and over the period since our contributors were children general standards of living have risen enormously.

ALICE ELDRIDGE

A gamekeepers daughter, as a child Alice Eldridge lived on the estates of two influential Sussex families - the Ashburnham's and Brassey's. She speaks about being a child in rural Sussex during the Edwardian years and of the very different life 'in service' when she left school and moved to Bexhill.

I was born at the gamekeeper's cottage at Netherfield in Sussex. I was the eldest. I was born 1898, the October. I was a seven month baby and Lady Ashburnham was with my mother when she was taken bad, she rode through the woods down Netherfield to Battle and fetched Dr Kendal. And Dr Kendal and her, she was on horseback, came back and they picked up an old lady as midwife. I was born with no hair, I was wrapped up and put in my father's boot and they said I would not make old bones.

I had three sisters. Nell, Mrs Philcox who lived in Catsfield, mother of Frank, there's 13 months different between me and her. Then we had Ann, four years between her, then brother Frank. When he was 16 he went to Canada and now he is in the nursing home *and I we*nt to see him yesterday. When I was 14 Dorothy came and she was always spoilt the love.

Father was a gamekeeper for the Ashburhams, but he got the sack from that, not because he wasn't good, but because he shot a fox which was eating his eggs he set in nests for pheasants, and the young pheasants, you see. That part of the estate didn't want the fox shot because of the fox hunting. You see, that's how it worked out.

When I was nine years old I cut the top off my finger and I had to walk to Battle from Catsfield. We were living there then, my Dad had changed work and was gamekeeper for Lord Brassey then. And I had to walk to Battle every other day for nine weeks for this finger. About three times I had my cousin walk with me. Sometimes down by Farthings Pond but mostly through Powdermill Lane.

It was a funny surgery at Battle, you know, you sat on the forms. One of the days a man came in and he said 'I be dying, I be dying. You know my wife is bad, so I thought I'd got the same thing. So I took

Mr Roberts, Alice Eldridge's father, and another Normanhurst gamekeeper

a dose of her medicine and I'm dying.' The doctor said 'You fool, don't you know one man's meat is another man's poison.' He mixed him up a dose of salts and mustard - there was a sink there - and he said 'here, drink this' and the man was violently sick and in the meantime there was me sitting waiting with my finger and that was that. The doctor said 'that will learn you, now you can clear it up yourself.'

Lady Brassey was our great charm. Lady Idina. My brother-in-law, Ron Furneaux, worked for them all his working life at Catsfield, you see. We had beautiful parties up at Normanhurst [Court] and that. I feel so sorry for the children now. I feel so sorry they don't know what luxury and happiness was then. They had the most beautiful Christmas trees and the young ladies that served us at the tea party were titled ladies. We'd been warned to be on our best behaviour at these parties. One year, Lady Helen Murray, she was Lady Helen Brassey, said to one of the boys, George Pankhurst, 'Oh have a cake little boy.' 'No thank you.' 'Oh do have one.' 'Don't you know when I say no, I mean it.' He got the cane the next day. I got sent to the corner because I laughed.

Mum and Dad lived then in the thatched cottage opposite the school in Catsfield, Home Farm. It was there an old farmer had his cows. He couldn't write himself so I used to write for him. 'Aler he wants you to do a bit of writing to make out a bill for the use of the bull' and I'd write 'for use of bull four shillings.' Aler was my nickname. Dad didn't never write very well. Very small he did, but he was a big man.

Our schoolmaster's name was Bleach, and Mrs Bleach she couldn't skin a rabbit but I could, so I was just crossing the road with a skinned rabbit in between two plates and a tramp came down the road and he stopped and he was suddenly sent flying right through the hedge. That was my father standing at the door to watch me. And my father said 'Thay'll learn you' and he went back indoors. And I went on with my rabbit in the dish and no one took a bit of notice, poor man and I don't think he ever said a word. Dad thought he was going to take the plate from me or something.

I went to Catsfield school from when I was four to 14. I was a good scholar, and they said they weren't going to let me leave for a little while. Anyway Mum said, 'Alice, you'll have to leave school because I want you to do some sewing for me.' 'Sewing', I said. I was

Normanhurst

a bit of a tomboy, you know. 'Yes' she said, 'I'm going to have another little baby. I said 'How do you know that?' And she pulled her nightdress tight round her stomach like that. She never said another word about how it come and when it was coming, we weren't supposed to know. And she was born the 28 November - my sister - she's Mrs Masters - and she was a lovely, lovely, lovely sister - she's always been like mine you know and she lives up in Jubilee Road in a little council flat. That was it.

I was about 15 when I originally left school. I never knew how my mother came to hear of this place, but there was a tin trunk all packed ready and everything and Mr Clifton, the carrier, came and brought me down to Cantelupe Road - to an apartment house. It was two big houses, 41 and San Remo, right on the corner of Bolebrook Road. I was not to do housework, not charing like. I was to learn cooking, that was the idea. But do you know for a fortnight I never touched a saucepan. It was all spent cleaning flues. She was a lady, a retired nurse, and she had her old mother and father living with her. They sort of had a basement place and they lived in that, like the ground floor and we, the maids (my cousin, who saw me when I was born, and another girl from Tunbridge Wells) we had the ground floor of the other house. My cousin and I worked it together. We had one other poor girl, May, she was only about 14, to do the scrubbing and get the coal. There were two waiters. They were youths, Germans, German waiters. They never had meals with us. And sex never came into things then. That never had been invented. Yes, we were young at that time but we were getting on.

I started work there at two shillings and six pence a week and no one else had any more than that and we had one half day off a week and every other Sunday, which we used to go to Catsfield when it was our day out. We were supposed to make up our wages in tips. There were four families that rented rooms in the two houses and they all had separate meals and they all had to be cooked at the same time - meat and two veg and puddings that all done by one o'clock in the day time.

One of the days dishing up these meals, one of the German waiters, was standing there - they both were named Jacob, never could understand them, they never spoke to us - and dropped something. Miss Levik, the lady, said 'more haste, less speed Jacob.' And he said 'Get my gun and I will shoot her.' Oh we had to hold him, we had to hold him it was terrible, terrible, and he went on like that.

When we got our half day holiday we would go to the Poppies. That was run by Will Tissington, and his wife May Holding - they were very nice. It was a concert party. Oh it was lovely. They used to have it down in the Polegrove or down in the Lawn, I can't remember which it was cause there were two, Poppies and another one. When we was on holiday we used to come down because we used to be in strictly at ten at night when we worked.

How did we get home to Catsfield? We walked back when we came on our holidays to Poppies, we used to walk and we used to sit on a seat. You know where Preston Lodge is, going up through Watermill Lane, and then higher up before you go down to the watermill, a place called Edgewood and between them two houses, on the bank there was a gypsy encampment. We used to get sixpence of chips and sit on the seat on the other side of the road by ourselves and they never took no notice and their old lurcher dog would come and sit with us. It was a proper road and we used to get home about 12 o'clock. It was such a treat to be out and we never knew any fear.

But to get back to these waiters. We never knew where they went. We never saw them come in at night. But they came down one day and they said 'The day has come.' And they went. They never waited for any money, they just left. And the next day war was declared; they were spies, and none of us knew. Kate said - the one that was illiterate - she said 'Jolly good riddance to you.'

When the war came it was marvellous and because soldiers and all that came. Canadians and Americans and all and we used to walk to Catsfield with them and come to no harm. We used to walk to the Gaiety Theatre [Hastings] and queue up and walk back - sit on the seat coming through what we called The Salts, between St Leonards and Bexhill, the waste bit, with the farm, cows and that on there now. And no trouble with any of them. Sex never was mentioned.

I went on working there, I stayed nearly eight years. Miss Levik had to give up, when things were beginning to get bad. Some tramp came in and we found her laying in the kitchen with her hair all cut off, some of the parts of her head, her hair was pulled out flesh and all, she had to give up. The old chap, old Mr Levik, he used to be after us. When the summer visitors left every little bit of soap they left he'd get and pack away, medicine bottles, he'd pack away, and when he died there were drawers full of tablets and soap and that.

I could cook those four meals and all those years we only had two shillings and six pence a week. Then I had a friend who wanted to go away for a holiday and she asked me if I'd take her work on for a fortnight, so I left the apartment house and it for an old colonel and his wife who used to live in Brassey Road in a flat and then I had a lovely time. I stayed with Colonel and Mrs Tealey and I got one pound a week then. I stayed with them till I got married. Then they went away to live down in Southsea and the Colonel said I broke up his home. But I had a lovely time. It wasn't like being in service because we lived together, worked together, like that.

Colonel Tealey, his daughter was Mrs Ronald Gibb. They had the Hotel Riposa, they were great bridge players. Opposite four Brassey Road where I lived was Sir Ernest and Lady Birch and one of their daughters was Mrs Ronald Cargill. She used to be a lovely lady and a great actress, getting up these concert parties and things. She had a little son and who do you suppose he was? Patrick Cargill, the actor. I had to mind him when the bridge parties and the croquet parties were on. He used to wear frocks and he used to turn all the cupboards out.

Then I got married, you see, in Catsfield Church. His name was Frederick. I got married at 27 and I'd known him all that time. We used to go to the circus and not like sweethearts, more like boy and girl companions, more than anything else. He was well thought of as a sportsman. He was the boy who used to come round with the greengroceries in Bexhill. He worked for Giggins, the greengrocer, used to be on the corner of St Leonards Road. He enlisted into the army then, he was in the Queen's West Surrey's and he got shell shocked and one leg shorter than the other, because he fell in a shell hole. Wasn't that they called injured though one leg was half an inch shorter for the rest of his life. He also served in the Home Guard in the Second War. He was on the emergency post office because he was painter and decorator then. His father was a shoe mender, shop in Wickham Avenue. Boot and shoe repairer.

I didn't get married till I was 27 because my real sweetheart was missing in the war and I always thought he would come back. Reg was a signaller in Lowthers Lambs and he was reported missing. He was last seen on enemy land which he had courageously reached and I couldn't think he never would come back. He was such a darling. He lived in Sidley. They had two sons, the other died of spotted fever and was buried at Harwich.

I got in with the Athletic Club a long long time before I was married. They gave me the clock on the mantle as a wedding present. 53 years I've worked there. When I started there was no Athletic Club. We collected for the building, it was a little tin hut, used as part of St Stephen's church. I used to go up, to what they called the Nimble Ninepences up the Old Town. I didn't dance, because I promised Reg I would never dance, and my job was always the washing up. I never did any running or anything like that. I did collecting for the different things. I never went swimming. I went in once and it stopped my breath and never went in again. I used to collect all sorts of things from the rocks. I tried all the things along there, the only one I never tried was the trampoline.

My own children? I had one bad miscarriage when a cat ran

between my legs, that was when I got registered as a foster mother I was so broken hearted. Another thing I used to go out with the district nurse. She lived in Cranston Avenue and I used to go out and help her with babies, unmarried mothers and like that, so I got to know a bit about babies being born and helping. One poor woman, I stood and held her leg up for an hour and half before her baby was born.

In the Second War I got three evacuees. Then I was evacuated to Stratford - left my cousin and Freddie here with the dog. I only stayed a little and then he had a bomb over here and I was so worried about them I came back and I got the children's parents to say that they could stay down there. They stayed down there but before long their mothers said they would rather they were killed up here than be miserable down there after I come back. So they come back here. The little girl, Sandy, she had such terrible fits so that her mother took her back to London. But the other two stayed six years. Judy went back to London but Ted stayed down here and when I had my ninetieth birthday this year I hadn't known anything about him for five years, and a card came on my ninetieth birthday from him with a five pound note. He lives in Wembley.

Then after the Second War we had a flat - two bedrooms, kitchen and scullery - its all altered now, but it was lovely. Twelve shillings and six pence a week. Then we moved into Eastwood Road. My cousin always made her home with me though she was 16 years older than me. She died in 1968 and my husband in 1969. But I was never lonely.

After the [Second] war he went back to his building for Mrs Bruce, and he was much thought of till he fell off this building, then he never worked again. I used to work for the Colonel when I was first married. Then I left and I had to go out to work because of Freddie not being able to work. I went to work daily for a dear lady called Mrs Webb and Lady Gidney who lived in Cantelupe Road and I used to do between them little housework. They were clairvoyants. They would have these things, unseen, and I would have to hold a photograph in the kitchen while they would talk - I used to hold this because that would bring one of their unseen ones from wherever they are, to them, they would tell them something. My husband was furious and he forbid me to go but I loved it and they were good to me.

51

We only went away, my husband and I, to London. Must have been the coronation or something, to see the decorations. Anyway he stayed at home with my sister-in-law and I went round the decorations with my brother-in-law. He never went away. He came down to see me when I was evacuated for the weekend, that was the only time. He wouldn't go. He would come out Christmas Eve to do the shopping and he would stand on the kerb with his back to the shops while we went in to do the shopping. He was difficult.

Bexhill has changed. There's a take it or leave it attitude in the shops now. You've got to have what they've made up, I mean, like a lump of cheese, done up in that cellophane. You don't want as much as that. Where you could go in and then get two rashers of bacon and get that. And mind you bacon was bacon then. Fat was to fry an egg in, now it's all too watery. I remember the drapery shop in Sackville Road. Yes, they were nice, they had two old ladies serving there. I used to wear corsets. Now I can't. That's what keeps your figure.

OLIVE WRIGHT

One of eleven children, Olive Wright tells of her childhood living in Holliers Hill and leaving school to work for Arscott's, the bakers. When only 15 she met her husband-to-be, a locally based soldier, a short while before he was sent to fight in the trenches in France.

I was born at Crowmere Cottage, Holliers Hill, Bexhill in 1900 and I had six sisters and two brothers. I was the middle child. Life was very hard for my mother. She had 11 children, two of them died.

We had quite a nice house with a big garden, a kitchen, sitting room and scullery. Four bedrooms and a dining room. Of course, when I was born we didn't have all this. It was two cottages and my father had them made into one so that there was more room. As the children came along we had to have more room. We had a room we used to call the library because we put all our books in it. In the kitchen we had a black range for cooking and a copper for washing and a mangle.

My mother had everything mapped out. Monday was washing day. Dad used to get up and light the copper and the fire and he would fill it from the rain tubs because that was soft water. Then he would call her at half past seven and she would start when he went to work. She would have bowls of rinsing water. Starch and a blue and then a rinse before the mangle. Everything was lovely and clean and white. Tuesday mornings she would iron, then Tuesday afternoons she would go down the grocers in Devonshire Road to get some of her shopping. Wednesday I can't remember what she did. Thursdays was shopping and she went into town. Friday was baking day. She baked all her own cakes and made all her own jam and lotions and wines. She had Earls bread. She had groceries delivered from somewhere in the Honies. Then when that closed she went to Turner's in Beaconsfield Road. I helped clean the spoons and forks and knives on Saturday and my sister and I used to argue about who's turn it was and my mother used to say, 'And what are you fighting over now?' and I had to clean the brass door handles and the fire irons. My mother used to polish the copper on Mondays after the washing until it shone beautifully. We used to do knitting and sewing. We was never allowed to go out.

If you sprained your arm my mother would get a piece of white rag then dig up a comfrey root. Then scrape the root onto the rag and it would go on your arm and it would stay there until it was cured. She made ointment from comfrey and plantain. That was for cuts and bruises. She would swear by that. If you had a cold or cough she made blackcurrant tea. It was almost worth being ill to have some of that, it was delicious. She made a lot of jam and wines and elder ointment and wine and dandelion wine.

A Gipsy woman came to the door once and my mother had passed on and the Gipsy said, I want to see the lady, not you, and my sister said that she had died and she went to her cart outside and bought her some flowers and said my mother had never turned her away she always gave her something, some old clothes that we had grown out of or something.

Dad was a market-gardener. We used to sell fruit and vegetables. He had two allotments and worked for himself. He employed other men. He also used to sell the fruit and vegetables to his customers in the town - not shops. Sometimes on Saturdays we used to help him out.

Oh, Bexhill was very different then. We didn't get a lot of traffic and where the hospital is there was a field. It used to belong to a man named Johnny Brook. And the other side was all fields - where now is Chantry Lane - all fields, right up through an iron gate, across the road, to the church. It was lovely. Most of my friends lived in the Honies. Springfield Road way. There used to be an old theatre down the bottom of Sea Road called the Kursaal. And the sea would come right up Sea Road when we had a storm. We used to go ice-skating on the pond where Church Vale Road is now. That was all fields. My father used to say 'don't go near it 'cause there's a well there.' A girl drowned herself it that pond. I remember the hospital being built. We used to give money for it. To get money for the hospital they had fairs in the fields there and fetes.

I went to school at St Peters in Barrack Road. One teacher was Miss Dunboy, and Miss Ratten, she was the Governess. I was five when I went to school and I left at fourteen. If we was naughty we had to put our pinafore over our heads and stand in the corner. All the girls wore pinnys. We might get slapped on the arm if we were naughty. The teachers were quite strict. We played stoolball. If we wanted to give up, say, one afternoon to play stoolball we paid so much money to play -perhaps three pence or something like that, not very much - but we paid a little bit of money. We had quite a big piece of grass to play on. We used to dance round the Maypole on May Day at school. We had bells on our legs and petticoats. It was a special day with a day off school.

On Sunday I had to go to Sunday School and church three times. I remember my elder sister used to take me, and we used to go up through fields to St Peter's Church. That was before they enlarged it and they were taking up the graves 'cause the graves came right up to the church and they had to take them up and my sister used to say, 'Look down there. There's a man!' The graves were covered up with wood but she used to frighten me. We went to church in the afternoon. My sister played the organ at home on a Sunday evening.

When I went to church we used to go on outings. We went to Cooden and took some food and tea up there. We went to Herstmonceaux Castle on a horse and cart with the Sunday School. We went to Ninfield or Catsfield. My mother came from Ninfield. They had a big farm out there we used to go and visit. We went to Church social evenings and lantern slides. I also joined the Band of Hope. You signed the Pledge not to drink. I signed the pledge umpteen times but I still like a drink! My father used to take us up on Eastbourne hills and he would take a cricket bat and some of his employees could come, Bob Hollins came. My father used to love cricket and the whole family went. We played cricket. That was a lovely day out. We didn't go away for a holiday.

We had marvellous Christmas's. We used to have things put in our stockings and then we would come downstairs and have breakfast. Our mother wouldn't let us have presents until we had had breakfast. She said 'If you get eating sweets you won't want no dinner.' So we had presents after breakfast. All the relatives were invited perhaps 14 or 15 people. I don't know how my mother did it all in those days. And she made all her cakes with best butter, never anything else but best butter and English meat, we was never allowed anything else. I know because I used to go to Pocock's in Old Town to get the meat before I went to school. My sister took a turn at going.

I left school just after the First World War started. Mr Arscott was a baker and he knew my father and he asked if us girls could go and work for him. So we went there. I helped to put the cakes on the tray to take into the shop. This was in St. Leonards Road. I rode a bicycle there and earnt about five shillings a week. I had to be there at half past seven in the morning till about six at night. I kept some of my money and gave some to my mother. I saved most of it up but I bought a few sweets. I was in the job for five years until I got married.

In the First World War we had some Canadians come over to Bexhill. They were billeted in private houses down Sea Road and places like that. We weren't allowed to associate with them. I didn't have any boyfriends till my husband came along. I met my husband in 1915 in the Baptist church. He was a soldier based by the golf course and he went to look round the town with a friend. He walked down Buckhurst Road and came across the Beulah Baptist church. They tossed up whether to go in and they saw two young ladies sitting on a bench. And he said to his comarade, 'That is the girl I'm going to marry.' We had never seen or spoken to each other then. Then my sister and I came out of the church. He had been talking to another girl in the church and asked who I was. She had said that I was engaged to be married. So he came up to me and said, 'Little missy, you engaged?' I looked at him and said, 'No I'm not! I'm only 15', and I walked down the road with him and he said to me, 'Will you see me on Wednesday?' I said 'yes, I suppose I can. I'll have to tell my mother.' (Because she was very particular what I did.) Mother said she supposed there wouldn't be any harm to see him. So I met him on the front where the Colonnade is. He said to me, 'I wanted to see you 'cause I'm going to France and I wondered if you would write to me.' So it was all done by writing. Then, after we had been writing for a long time, he said 'would you be my girlfriend?' I supposed it would be alright because I might never see him again.

He was badly gassed. I had this thing come through the post - 'I have been gassed' I didn't know but he was given up almost for dead. But he got my letter which said I would be his girlfriend and they said he went to sleep that night for the first time since he had been gassed. The nurse noticed a change in him and told the doctor about the letter. I don't know, it gave him fresh hope I suppose. He kept that letter with him always. He was sent to York to recover.

I hadn't heard much from him while he was away then one Sunday night I came out of church and he was standing outside and said he would be stationed near Brighton and he would be able to see me weekends. He used to stay with my grandma. He was in an office then and he said 'I'm going to India and I'll be there for perhaps six or seven years. Do you think we could get married?' I said I would marry him and he must see my father. Then I had letters from the Army to say I must be inoculated. I had to go to London and then Southampton and got a big boat and I can remember standing on the deck watching England go away and thinking, 'I wonder if I'll ever see old England again.' I sent a postcard to my mother to say I was sailing.

REG CANE

Reg Cane's account reveals how his family tried to make ends meet when his father died in 1910, provides some fascinating insights into the sights and sounds of Bexhill during and after the First World War, and describes his key role in the history of Bexhill's noteable Athletics Club.

I was born here in Bexhill in the two little Holly Cottages in Belle Hill on 5 February 1902. Holly Cottage was on the right hand side after the sweep going up to the Old Town. There were lots of what were fishermens' cottages, like where they used to have nets and that sort of thing. They made a single cottage out of it, Applefield Cottage I think, which goes out on to Millfield Road. Then we went to Beaconsfield Road.

My father was van driver for Cave Austin the grocers up in the Old Town Bexhill, under the Jubilee Clock. He kept his horse at Cave Austins, there was a small yard on the side of it. He worked there for 11 years. They had a very bad fire there I remember and he had to go out in the night and get the horse and van free from down in the yard. I must have been about four. My father got a certificate awarded 23 May 1905 for best groomed and cared for horse in Bexhill Horse Parade without bearing or tight reins. Then unfortunately my father died of lung trouble, consumption, in January 1910 just after the Christmas. He was only 32 and mother only 30. Sitting in his van, it was one of those circular hooded vans open back and front, with a through draught all the time you see. Mind you Holly Cottage was built right into the bank, in a damp bank. There wasn't all this damp proofing.

My poor mum was left with three of us. No widow's pensions, no nothing those days. From then, 1910 we moved down here to Windsor Road. She came from Peasmarsh, near Rye. Her name was Lucy Filmer. I've got their wedding certificate, must have been 1898. Ma married when she was 18. That clock on the mantlepiece was a wedding present. Dad was brought up in Uckfield, his father was a blacksmith and he worked till he was over 80 they tell me. His wife,

Left to right, Winnie Cane, H H Bird, Beattie Bird, Charlie Cane, Lucy Bird, Reg Cane. July 1914

Old Gran, she didn't die till she was about 93.

I had one older brother, Charlie. He worked here at Stewart Apps when it was a sports outfitters in St Leonards Road. He was helpful in the club early on - the Athletic Club. He married and he's down in Bridgewater and he still keeps smart and bright. They evacuated during the war when there was a threat of invasion. I also had a sister who died some while back. She had one daughter Mrs Irene Crowhurst and eight sons - she made up for mine. All I've dealt with is other people's families.

My mother rented the house in Windsor Road. It was actually two flats and my mother being a widow and the other person upstairs was a widow. There was a passage came through this back living room so upstairs could come down and use the scullery. Then there was a front room. The house, one of a terrace, was actually built in 1887. Rent nine shillings covered rates and everything for my mother and three of us.

She worked. I think the tram fare used to be about two pence in those days. But she didn't always get it, so she walked from here right away to the top of Dorset Road to Ebor School - the boys school run by Mr Brown. She used to work up there for two shillings a week and if it was charing or scrubbing - they had wooden floors - she got two shillings and six pence. My mother was out at work all day so when we came back from school we just hoped there was a meal of some sort. Miss Huxley took it over and it became Ancaster Gate School.

I went to the Downs School after St Barnabas at the infants when we was still at Beaconsfield Road. My brother went to Reginald Road School. I was sent right down to the Down's. I went to Sunday school that's where I got this urge to do gym. When I first moved down here when I was only eight I used to go to Sunday School in the Victoria Hall and you see there they had a pair of rings and a trapeze and you could just imagine swinging from the rings and catching on to the trapeze. I used to pray. I used to get this little tingling in my ears there whenever I looked up there, cause I was no age then.

Life was difficult. I must have started work when I was about 11. I left school at 13, you could then. You left at 14 but providing you put in a certain percentage of attendances you could leave at 13. Even then I was doing three different jobs before I left school. I done a paper round for Jillo, newsagent, opposite Woolworths, down Devonshire Road for two shillings a week; then this cobbler's round in the evening; and each Saturday I worked all day for Pratley on what is now the Midland Bank on the corner of Western road and Devonshire Road. I was just taking out greengroceries you see.

The cobbler's job was for school repairs, all up round Hastings Road - they were all private schools. This little cobbler down opposite the steps by Sainsbury's there, you know those little shops, old fashioned places tumbling down they've done them up re-built them like Georgian, beautiful little places now. Well the second one from the end was Jim Cornford. I've got a photo of him standing out there, cobbler, he used to take in these repairs from all private schools so even at that age I had a huge black bag of shoe repairs to take back every day and another lot to collect.

Bexhill was all schools before the last war. In Hastings Road nearly every building was a school. Devonshire House, that was a boys school. There was Boscobel, that was boys and girls. So many of them. They come into the town but they were generally paraded in groups in their uniforms, with a teacher all under control.

They were hard time inasmuch in that every morning about every third week apart from going up to the shop and taking them out you had to go and collect the papers from West Station, you had to be there extra early then. Not Central Station. These papers always come in on the Crowhurst line at West Station and we had to push this great wicker basket like postman had for parcels with a big wheel we had to get them back to the shop for sorting, before the lads come in. I went straight to school from the shop - fainted a time or two - you're running all the way.

The school was not on the Downs then. The troops had taken that. It's one of my awful memories of going past the school up to what was Garth Place in those days on top of the Downs. It was run by Blasnik a German as a German boys school before the war. That's why it was suspected on the outbreak of war. They found stuff there and of course he was interned and Canadian troops took it over. Last war the Council took it over.

My vivid recollection was always in the early days of the First World War, you see, Belgium got over run didn't it? And we took in a terrific lot of Belgian refugees all round the town that had to come away from the war zone and they were, every morning, waiting for their plates outside the railings of the school playground - getting food from the troops. We had to pass the school that we were due to go to and the troops had it. They fed all their bits and pieces to the Belgian refugees who used to line the railings of the playground.

It was during the First World War that we used to have a woman lodging with us. We found room, cause we had to use the front room for a bedroom for us lads you see. I know we only had the two rooms but I think Mrs Cornford the woman upstairs let my mother have one of her bedrooms. She [the lodger] was chummy with the quartermaster-sergeant from the Cooden camp - he had charge of all the stores - QMS Lyons his name was. It was him that got me these boxing gloves. He got them in from the camp. I used to go to Cooden and watch some of their boxing shows and they knew I was keen.

We used to go across the road to 105 opposite and make use of the gloves in the loft we cleared for us over there. Old Ashdown, old bearded boy, down in the yard had it. We rented it from him. Candles set fire to the cobwebs. We used to pick the football team. We had friendly games against Service Invalids. There used to be a voluntary aided hospital at Cooden you see, and the troops used to come down. We could only get friendly games around the district. There was no organised football league during the war. Of course at the back of us, the stable yard, was the Empire Laundry. Old Mary Stampton, she also ran a football team and used to give us a game. We played over in Cranston Avenue.

We went to Cooden by tram. Only a tram track. Overhead wire, terrible bit of road. Soldiers were camped up top of the hill of Cooden Sea Road, on the mound, the Mount was an old property which has been developed. Lowthers Lambs, the South Downs formed two battalions. Colonel Lowther was a big noise.

Just your main track up through the London Road to Sidley. It wasn't made up roads as such. The Pelham Hotel was there. There was a railway station where the garage was. Last train to Crowhurst was never later than quarter to nine. Till Beeching shut all that area.

While we were there up in the loft the troops came in and claimed four out of his [Ashdown's] six horses and commandeered them. That was the only transport the troops had when they first established out at Cooden. Ashdown used the horses for heavy contracting work instead of trucks and vans and lorries, just horses and carts. Like Carey's used to be, road construction, they had quite a number

Some of Lowthers' Lambs' at Cooden Camp, 1914

and Mephams up here, he had about eight different vans and horses in the yard behind this house. I remember them going through our arch [between 80 and 82]. You could tell each horse. They had a certain patter of their hooves going up and down. There was King, there was Buller, there were two or three different ones. You couldn't mistake them going up and down with a different patter.

There were two flats over the stables up there [at the back of Reg Cane's house]. Where the big Fludes got his carpet place there now it used to be like a big 'L' looking down the arch and that was two little flats, a little old dear was living there. It was all heavy horse and vans in those days. There was a bigger arch next door, taller and wider as they used to get one of the big oil tankers, even these were pulled by horses, oil vans, carting petrol and oil, paraffin - those days there wasn't the road traffic.

There used to be two or three blacksmiths. One at the end of the passage at the back of Windsor Road [where it] goes down into Terminus Road. Now there a bus shelter in Terminus Road, right opposite that there was a blacksmith. I think he was Stephen Turner. Up at Sidley there was another Turner, George Turner, where the

DIY is now. Up in the Old Town of course, just as you start sweeping down Sea Road on that left hand side as you go up before you come to the shops, was a blacksmith. I used to love to stand there, because all my private schools were up in the old town, Hastings Road, Dorset Road, Penland Road. I'd go into the next shop, Pasines the bakers. If I'd got a few coppers I'd get a bit of this chocolate Swiss roll in there, this stale stuff, you'd get a big chunk for three pence and stand in there and watch the smithy. Oh when the old sparks were flying it was beautiful. Old Jim and George Wimborne, I think. George was still a blacksmith down the Corporation Yard when it all packed up.

There were a lot of children in Windsor Road and we all played together and that's how we formed the [Athletics] Club you see. The club really originated from the stable loft, then the Malet Hall. We kept trying to go down into the Malet Hall - down the bottom of Belle Hill, what they call House of the Lord, opposite the fish and chip shop. They had the church up top and quite a nice hall down below, see they had jumble sales and all. They had a scout troop attached to it. One of the school mates, Les Manson's, father was caretaker for the Malet Hall, you see. We used to creep in there on excuse of helping the old caretaker and used a bit of these scouts' gym stuff. When the club started first after using the stable loft across the road, that's where we used to be able to get in once or twice a week.

Old Reverend Maycock was rector of that as it comes under St Peter's Parish. So we had to get his permission to go into there to help the caretaker as an excuse to use some of this gym gear. Twice he caught us and he was so frightened we'd be hurting ourselves cause they had nice rings hanging from the ceiling and a trapeze. We went to see the vicar the Reverend Maycock. We could very well have bolted and nothing would ever have happened - cause there was a noise on this great clanging bell. He was good enough to come to the door and have another chat. 'Good heavens' he said, 'I've turned you out twice, you must be very keen. Don't you think you could get about 12 lads together - 12 to 20 - I could let you go in there one evening a week from boys clubs.' So that's how it we started down there. Sure enough we got 10 or 12 names in quick time but we couldn't get anyone to be responsible for us but we nominated one of the taller lads, young Bill Barnum down the road here. But by the time we went back and saw Maycock he said 'with all the luck in the world I've been able to get someone that will come and stand in with you, each evening that you go down there.' That was old Edwin Bailey who was a butcher up in Holliers Hill opposite the casualty department. I think it is a son-in-law of his who runs it now. Another man who helped in those early days was a very good character, ice cream man, Swiss, known all round the town, fellow called Bob Graber, was a very good gymnast.

We were in the archway loft in 1917, with the cobwebs and candle grease. We didn't have to pay for the Malet. The Malet must have been on the demobilisation of the troops in about 1918, as they used to come in down there from the Queens' pub. I was still crazy on boxing. As the chaps got demobbed these hawker chaps that used to follow us an' kid us along on our boxing you see, they were all barrow boys down by the Sackville Arch, green groceries and fruit. All the week. This side of the arch, opposite, there's a bollard in the middle of the road, all along where there's that big awning at the end of the toilets. There used to be about six barrows they allowed there and these hawkers used to be down in that yard with us so they knew of us, that's why they got interested in our boxing.

But then we went to the back of the fire station in Amherst Road in 1922. We had Hamilton's garage. Hamilton's is still there and we had to get eight public people to stand guarantor for us for the rent as we were only a bunch of youngsters. Then we got funds for the new building for the Athletic Club. Frank Bending was mayor. Got it ready when Munich happened [about 1938], everyone questioned us going ahead. Tom Wallace was the builder at the bottom of Buckhurst Road where Sea Scouts are, he took it on and we had it built just on the outbreak of war. It was completed but we had put down temporary cement floor. We went in in April '46. When we moved from Amherst Road we only had an open lorry to take our gear and it was a wet night, a wet trip. I'm president now, but in those days I was just club leader. For over 40 years I was club leader.

Before the Second World War I had club in the evenings and camping first weekend of May till first weekend of October. Tents could be left there all the time, and you knew that spot of ground was dry. Up at Highwoods. Captain Francis Gunn who used to be quite a big noise in Bexhill he let us use it - this Edwin Bailey he rented the Highwoods from Captain Gunn. He used to let us go camping that is before there was a Highwoods. We were keen on our gym and

Highwoods Camp, 1934. Left to right, Reg Cane, R Bryant and W Twigge

Highwoods Pool, 1934

walked the bars. When war broke out so many of the lads were mobilised for the territorial army. Camps go back to 1926. Gunn let us use if after poor old Bailey had to pack it up you see. He had a big piggery up there. Then he fell ill and we carried on. Charley Gulliver took it over, a big theatrical man from London. He made a pool for us, often used to bring his theatrical friends up. We love to go up there each autumn. I can still recognise now part of natural woodland. Tidier than it used to be now the conservation people have tidied it up. Our pool for the camp was a mud hole - now all the site has been demolished. Even had a boxing ring up in the woods. That day the Duke of Gloucester came to visit the camp - we got him to lay a foundation stone.

When I left school in 1915 I must have started full time at Jimmy Miner's in St Leonards Road cause my brother left there and came up to Mephams in the yard here as a stable boy. It was where there is a computer shop now on the corner of Eversley Road and St Leonards road that used to be a gents outfitters. In the shop I was errand boy.

Reg Cane

They didn't do repairs on the premises. It was new footwear. I was itching to leave and get on the building. I was so keen on boxing in those days and early days of the gym. So I wanted to do something more strenuous you might say. But anyway Jimmy Miner died and then Mrs Miner died and I got started plastering - 1924 I suppose. Baber and Edwards gave me the chance. He was the father of the man who blew up the viaduct at Crowhurst. Then I went plastering and sub-contracting on my own with two gangs and I was never out of work. They came to me and I didn't have to go chasing. Tom Wallace and Larkin between them two. Larkin came in from near Tunbridge Wells. I had an invite for the fiftieth anniversary of his firm in Bexhill at Moor Hall.

Not so much a town for retired people before the war. Some Indian army retired. Several of our mayors old Turner Lang, Mr Bowery, Mr Cuthbert, all came from overseas, sort of government officials. I didn't get involved in local government. They always had a go at me, especially the Labour Party which I joined. I'm a member. I've thought of the local council but then I've been so one track minded towards the club. You see every evening, all of my evenings were there, each day of the week there was something on.

Bexhill has got more congested. I remember the De La Warr and the roof being open, they should open it if possible - such a feature should be used - and coastguard cottages and the Colonnade. There were the big buildings too. One of the lads was page boy at Marina Court. Eleven flats there. Metropole was always a headache. It paid its way, but eventually we even had club annual meetings there or our whist drives nearly 100 tables or in the Old Town church hall. Sackville Hotel, that was a first class hotel. I remember Sir John Simon coming down. He spoke at the Commercial Associations annual dinner at the Sackville, and saying 'to increase the old age pension would bring bankruptcy on the country.' I always remember just before war, it was ten shillings a week and then within a week we were at war and spending millions. We could find it for the war, but you couldn't find it to increase the pension.

I'm a nut case for the sun. Love to go and sit down there on the beach and stretch out in the sun. At one time there was no public bathing, no undressing, an offence. Right up to the far end towards the west there was none of that beach washing. Beach used to be down there and they had this iron ladder you used to go down and they had canvas awning projecting so you could dress and undress. When you walked, it was nearly all sand out to the sea. There were sand artists and you looked over the promenade and threw coppers down onto their platters. The iron gates on the promenade were dismantled. Gulliver took them down and had them on his bowls green for a while. [They were removed by the Council in 1913 and subsequently erected on the bowling green.] Possibly during the war they took them for scrap iron.

69

PERCY CYRIL DOWLING

Mr Dowling's story describes many of his adventures as a boy growing up in Bexhill. In an often amusing way he shows how important the town was as a seaside resort in the first few decades of the century.

I was born on September 2 1905 and went to school where the Library is at the moment. That was the Infant's School - boys downstairs, girls upstairs. We had to write on slates on those days. Mrs Willard, the barber's wife, she was the school mistress there.

After two years I went to St Barnabas' School, which was in Reginald Road. 'Caley' Poulton was the headmaster. He was a big churchman. He was a very good man as a teacher, very good. He was greatly respected, all the old boys used to come back, you know - sailors and soldiers and all that sort of thing. They all came to see Caley. You got the cane if you misbehaved. He was quite strict. But Mitchell, the man directly under Caley, he was a villain. He would hold your cheek - like that - and smack your side of the ear with the other hand! He was a vicious bloke. Frisby was all right he was a nice man.

Bexhill was very nice for a schoolboy to be in then. When we got to St Barnabas' School there used to be West and Somebody's greengrocers, that would be next to Tate's. Of course, as a schoolboy, apples on the front were pretty tempting. I went back and grabbed an apple and it was a pyramid. Of course, I grabbed one low down! I didn't stop to see, I bolted to school. But he came round to the school and I got a caning for that from Caley.

We had a boy there who he was a bit of a lad, and a bit of a thief. Eventually, he got had-up and he got the birch. But never ever again did he steal! The birch cured him completely. It was administered in Cantelupe Road [police station] but I don't know who did it. I suppose one of the sergeants.

If a policemen caught you doing a silly thing he would just clip you 'side the ear. If he was carrying his cape on his shoulder, he would fling the cape round the back of your head and give you one. In the old cab days you would sit on the axle. There was plenty of room but if someone yelled 'Whip behind!' the old cabby would flick the whip over, and give you one round the face. Well they didn't

Percy Cyril Dowling, aged about 12

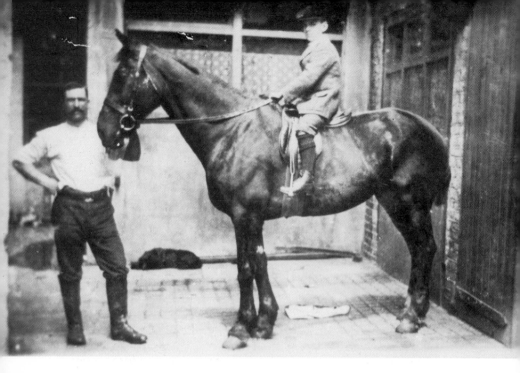

Percy Cyril Dowling on a horse at the Cunningham and Sabin's stables

travel very fast, you could sit on and have a ride.

My dad worked for Cunningham and Sabin which is now Courts. He drove a horse and van for delivery for Sabin and at the back there was a riding stable. So I got friendly with Jimmy Shipp, who was the head chappie there. When they took horses out to Hastings Road or Little Common, if they hadn't got a groom to take the other three - if they were taking six out, one man could ride one, and lead two, you see - I used to ride one and lead two. Then I had to kick me heels for an hour and a half just to get a ride back.

But I paid for that once, didn't I. Mr Gill who used to look after the Fire Brigade horses down there, that's when they had moved to Sackville Mews, behind the old Sackville Hotel. Gill said to me one day 'Do you want a little job, Perce?' I said 'I don't mind.' I don't know what the horse's name was, but he said 'Old so-and-so wants shoeing. Will you take it to Turner's Forge?' He said 'You can't ride him, he's too wide for your little legs, you'll have to lead him.' So I took him to Turner and waited while he was shod. I had just got into Station Road, through the Town Hall Square, when the maroon [fire alarm] went. The horse galloped back to the stables in Middlesex

Road, you see. What with me dangling off the bridle, and him stamping. He stamped both the toes off me shoes, and he didn't bust me toes, but be bruised them badly. But I got highly commended by old Gill, because I never let go the damned things, I stopped with it!

In those days, even in winter, we used to play out in the street, under the street lamp. All sorts of things, kids' games. Favourite trick was to get a bit of string and tie two door-knobs together, then knock at the doors and run away! I remember doing it to George Britt's father, and their next door neighbours, the Winbournes. I tied Winbourne's cord on the door and I was just going to tie it on Britt's door, when Britt opened the door - so all I got was a smack side the ear!

We were living in Cornwall Road, then, when I was a boy. It was a marvellous road. Plenty of youngsters. I can remember a lot of the people in the road. Alf Burgess was a plumber. Tom Warren and Bill Warren, brothers, they were both carpenters. Then we had Mr Cushlin, the German, who was the head waiter at the Sackville - he was interned during the 1914-18 war. They had three children, Amy, Kathleen and Gus.

I can tell you a good story of Gus. Ashworth's wife was a dressmaker and that's how I came to work for Jack Ashworth through Mrs Ashworth. I used to take her dressmaking parcels to Dorset Road and Manor Road and that area. In those days I had a four-wheeler [go-cart], a box on four wheels. So of course, we had Gus in the box and me sitting on the back treadling like the Devil with me feet. We delivered the parcels all right, and coming down Dorset Road we tipped over. Two French ladies (who were customers of Mrs Ashworth's) saw us and took Gussy in, and tied his head up which he had a little cut on - left poor Looby standing out in the road with the truck! So I had to scramble home to Cornwall Road with the truck, and I got down the alley behind home, and got the old truck over the wall. I was just going in the door when I heard a rumpus. It was Mrs Cushlin at the front door after my skin because I had injured her Gussy.

Any rate, Bill Warren, was a carpenter, he heard it, and he came across and he said 'Look, you can't blame one boy and leave the other one out if you have a little accident.' He said to Mrs Cushlin 'You want to go off home and mind your own damned business!.' So with that I got away with that one.

There was one trick I didn't get away with. We lived near the park. It was a great thing in the park in my school days to wade across to the island and take ducks eggs. I went across one day and I got some eggs, and while I was picking up the eggs, standing in the water, the park-keeper came along. He shouted 'I'll have your hide my boy!' you know, and I had to scramble across the pond and get out. I had got the eggs wrapped up in me jersey in front of me, you see. Of course, I slipped in the water and smashed the eggs which ran all down me trousers and they stunk and made me a hell of a mess. He never caught me - but my mother did!

We got the wanderlust. We started at 53 Cornwall Road and finished up in 26. The joke was, before we left 53, my mother and father were offered the house for £150 and they could not even afford that in those days. The houses in Cornwall Road were biggish, two rooms downstairs, and a kitchen and scullery; three up and then you had the attic - but of course, you never had a bathroom.

My mother always had lodgers. Of course, in the summer she had holiday people staying. We had one family who used to come for two weeks every year. He was in the hat business, and my father and I always used to click a new cap every year! It was hard work. Very often, my mother would have two families - one in the front room, and one in the rear room, and the two bedrooms front and rear upstairs.

In my young days, when my mother was dishing up the meal, I used to trot along with it, so she only had to come to the door and take it off me. It was visitors first and family second. She cooked for three families - us, and the two others. All on a coal range. When I eventually got to the gas industry in 1926 I got a gas-cooker for my mother and fitted it and to my knowledge she never ever did use the oven. She used the top but never the oven. She always cooked on the kitchen range.

We had some good hotels then and roads like Cornwall Road and Albert Road and Linden, those sort of places were all boarding houses and that sort of thing. We had the Kursaal, the Lawn - which was a concert party at the rear of Marina Court. We had the Poppies in the Park. Then of course, we had the Playhouse and the Bijou. Later on we had the Ritz and someone had a bit of a cinema down by the York Hotel. And, of course, we had the skating rink [Buckhurst Road], the rollers. I was fortunate. My father worked there for a bit.

74

So I had lots of skates. It was a popular place. They had an orchestra of sorts - suspended above the spectators and the rink. It was a hall with a wooden floor.

We boys used to go to the cinema - you paid if you had to. The dodge was, if the old boy, the commissionaire bloke, had the side door left open, you could nip down the track there and in the exit door. Dogs were not allowed in the cinema. Bert King from Linden Road, he had a dog, Trimmer, and wherever Bert went the dog went. If we went to the cinema on a Saturday morning he would say to Trimmer 'You stop outside then, boy.' But we had no sooner got in the cinema than Trimmer would be sitting in between our legs. Old Earl [the commissionaire] would up and take him out - but he would get back in again. Marvellous dog.

In the school holidays I worked for the Bexhill Bathing Company. It was right opposite the putting course. They were the first bathing huts ever to have a shower. I used to take the tickets at the huts, wash towels, we had a wooden thing there, with a scrubbing board and a wringer. I remember, it used to be Hudson's Soap we used, in packets. I worked for a man there called Ashworth. I used to take his midday meal from his home in Cornwall Road to the bathing station.

Buxton's Bathing Station, circa 1920

Invariably, he would draw a cartoon on the napkin surrounding the plate and sent the lot back; until one day I suddenly thought 'That's ridiculous to waste all this good food.' So I used to go down in The Hollow [an area of open ground where the West Parade flats are now], undo his plate, eat his meal and take his empty plate back to his wife - who was delighted to think that he had eaten his dinner!

I had one good incident there, which is rather nice. Ashworth was away for the moment. I was in the hut from which we sold the tickets, chocolate, minerals and all sorts of things. A couple came off the ramp from the bathing huts, to go up the steps to the sea front, when the woman's knickers dropped off! So with presence of mind, I said to the lady 'Step in here', which she did. I shut the cabin door. She had snatched up her knickers and was able to go in, and put them on. She gave me half a crown and they went off. Half a crown was worth having!

I remember most of the tips in those days were coppers and I used to take them to old Mr Tutt who had a pet shop in Western Road. He was always delighted to change my coppers for silver coin, so almost daily I used to go in to Mr Tutt and change money up.

The town was very busy in summer. We always had a military band which used to play at the bandstand at the Colonnade before the war. We lads used to sit on that piece facing the sea you know, because it was always crowded, hundreds of people. I remember in 1914 when war was declared the band was playing. When they got the news they immediately packed up and went out of the town.

Of course, then all horses were confiscated. When they were getting ready from the Drill Hall they were all staked along the Down on long running ropes. The owner's wife at Sabin's, they confiscated her own personal horse, but instead of letting it go she had it done away with, she would not let it go for war.

In the 1914-18 War, Cornelius the coach-builder's son, Eric, he started selling papers in Cooden Camp. The camp was where Cooden Mount was in those days, which of course is now all built on. I have no idea what I got paid for doing the paper round. At that time I had just learned to ride a bike. So Eric said 'Would you like to come out to Cooden Camp with me - you get a damned good breakfast.' So I said I wouldn't mind. So we used to cycle out there and go our separate ways in the huts. By the time I had finished I had a breakfast in the private's quarters and I had also had another breakfast in the sergeants' quarters. They were the Canadians.

The South Africans were there at one time. They had that bear that they took with them everywhere they went. A great thing! I have been near it, but not too near! It was always chained up in the sort of guard-room at the entrance to the camp.

At the bottom of Clavering Walk there used to be a club. They took that over and that was a VAD [Voluntary Aid Detachment] place. I used to take papers in there, and go through the wards, and sell papers.

During the First World War you used to queue for butter, margarine and that sort of thing. I remember once in Cornwall Road when the Zeppelin come over, coming out of England and out across the Channel it was so low you could see the blokes standing in there! We were too interested to be afraid. We stood there, gawping at the thing. It was a terrific great long thing. There were no anti-aircraft guns in the town like the Second War. Apart from the restrictions, and the loads of soldiers in the town, it was quite ordinary. You would go about in the ordinary way, there were no air raids or things like that. You could hear the guns from France - a rumble you know.

I started work just after the First World War. I went to Marina Court. I was to start at half-past-seven; cleaning the corridors and places. Then the refuse would be put on the landing, I would take the lift up to the three floors, one floor at a time, pick up all the bins and things with rubbish in - and the coal buckets - take them downstairs, get rid of the rubbish, fill the coal buckets and deliver them to the four flats on each floor. I worked from half-past-seven till 12. Then one day I would go home for lunch and come back and work till four. The next day I would start at half past six and work till 12, go home to dinner, come back at two and finish at ten! That was every other day - Saturday and Sunday as it came. I remember my first Christmas there. I made £25 in Christmas tips, and that was a lot of money in those days.

I had to operate the lift. That was controlled and run with water. You operated it with a rope, which came through the bottom of the cage to the top. All you did was pull it to start her going up, hold the rope, and let it flow through your hands. When you wanted to stop, you just turned your wrist, and that stopped it wherever you were. It was a matter of getting used to when to turn your wrist, to get it level with the floor. It was quite easy, but when it needed attention you knew because invariably you would go up all right. But you would start to come down, and you would lose control on the rope entirely and go down with a bump!

There were 14 flats, two on the hall floor and four on each of the three floors. There used to be a lady in the first one; the door opened onto the hall. From the first night I worked there, she called me in the evening, and said, was I the new boy? What was my name? Would I like some supper? I said yes, I would, thank you very much. From then on until I left, every night that I was on till ten I had the same meal as she had, no matter what. Even if it was a bit of salmon, I still had it. I never washed up. I offered the first night and she said no, it didn't matter.

I never thought anything of those hours, you know. On Sunday evenings in the summer, I used to stand outside, and listen to the Salvation Army band playing at the top of the road there by the [Bexhill] Club. They would start off at the Citadel, and they would play at Buckhurst Place, by what was then the grocers. Then they would come under the arch, and up Western Road and down Devonshire Road and play by the club. I stayed about a year and a half at Marina Court. Then I went and became a plumber's apprentice at Hodgkinson's.

PAUL ALLAN HODGKINSON

Mr Hodgkinson's father owned an ironmonger's shop in Devonshire Terrace, and this account tells something of being a child in a relatively well-off family - including the importance of private schooling, the church and music, in everyday family life.

My father's name was Paul Hodgkinson. He was born in 1866 and came to Bexhill in 1900. My mother was Jessie Asher Taverner and she was born in 1870. The Taverners were a musical family, her nephew John was the composer. My grandparents owned a house in Eversley Road from 1897 and they came there for their holidays. That's how she met my father. They were a large family and as Granny had a wooden leg Mother took charge of them all. At the bottom of Sea Road was a bath chair for hire, drawn by a donkey. The man who owned it and ran it was a Mr Flea, but he always called himself Flay. Granny used to go out in this vehicle. I remember the bath chairs, wicker ones for summer and big black ones with hoods for protection against the weather for use in winter. Father's family were farmers, except for his youngest brother, who was a chemist. Father had been an apprentice ironmonger at Lymington, Hampshire, and an improver at Haines Bros., Maidstone. My brother Jack also trained with this firm.

Father bought the ironmongers shop in Devonshire Terrace, now called Devonshire Square, from a man called Graveny. When my parents married in 1900 they lived in a maisonette above number four. I remember we had a room called the nursery there. At number five there was a room used by the Bexhill Telephone Exchange before it moved to Buckhurst Road. My father later bought this property and also extended into Western Road with the furniture business.

At number four we had a living-in maid. There were five children in the family: Muriel born 1901; John, who was always called Jack, born a year later; myself born 1905; then three years after that Mildred; and last Spencer who was again three years younger. He was born in 1911 and it was about this time we moved to a house on the corner of Clifford Road and Station Road, it was a large one but Mother still only had one living-in maid. There's a block of flats built

Hodgkinson's ironmongers shop, Devonshire Terrace, before 1909

on this site now.

In the summer holidays we sometimes used to let the Clifford Road house. Very often we went to Tunbridge Wells, it was very convenient for father because he could come down to Bexhill to see about the business. [Bexhill at this time had a direct rail link via Bexhill West Station with Tunbridge Wells.] We got to know Tunbridge Wells quite well. We used to have a house then, sometimes we went into rooms. I remember we went into rooms in Mount Zion, near the station, and then we had a house at the northern end of the town, Culverton Park Road.

I went to Miss Earle's school, where the Bexhill Club is now. It later moved to Wickham Avenue on the left-hand side. I remember I learnt German there at an early age. Later on I got a prize for this language when I was at Cranbrook. I didn't play games until I went to Ebor School. Originally it was at the bottom of Sea Road on the left-hand corner, then it moved to Dorset Road. I think the building later became Ancaster Gate School, and it's now demolished. I used to walk to school along Manor Road with Ronnie Arscott, the son of the original Jethro and his first wife. He had the baker's shop in St Leonards Road. Later Jack and I both went to a school in Springfield Road, St Leonards, just above the Buchanan Hospital. Sometimes we walked back from there over the fields. When I was about 16 I went to Cranbrook. Spencer eventually went there too. Jack stayed on at Springfield. I can't think where the girls went to school. I suppose I changed school quite a lot of times.

During the 1914 War the Canadians were billeted in Bexhill and one winter the boating pool in the Park was thickly iced over up to the island at the Wickham Avenue end. Everyone who could went there to ice skate and of course the Canadians relished the idea of skating. It's the only time I remember Egerton Park lake being frozen over to the extent it was then. I had new skates but ricked my ankle the first time I tried them out.

There was a firing range on South Cliff about opposite Southcourt Avenue. The Canadians used the cliff embankment as background for target practice and fired from the west end. My brother Jack and I collected lead bullets, perhaps they were revolver bullets, I'm not sure, and melted them down in a pan over the fire in our bedroom when we had chicken-pox. That was when we lived at Clifford Road. I don't remember my parents being cross with us or worried, everything was quite regulated and I'm surprised Father and Mother didn't object.

Horse-drawn vehicles were everywhere and it was not unusual to see a herd of cattle being driven up Western Road to board cattle trucks in a siding in Devonshire Square at the end of the station platform. I remember one horse in particular in Devonshire Square as it had a tracheotomy hole in its neck as it had difficulty in breathing and it had a little metal tube in it's throat so it breathed through this.

The trams were a nuisance when we lived in Devonshire Square. You see there weren't bogey wheels on them so it made a bit of a noise on the rails when they went round a corner. And of course when they got to what was the Hastings Gasworks they went across the fields straight ahead, it was a bit rocky. Manor Road was even steeper than the Bulverhythe Hill but they got up that alright. I remember the trolley pole came off the rails under Bopeep Arch one day and my brother was left holding it.

During the First World War some cars used gas instead of petrol and could fill large bags on the roof of their vehicle. They got their gas from the gasworks at the corner of De La Warr Road and also from the Marina Garage at the bottom of Eversley Road.

Where the telephone exchange now stands in Buckhurst Road there was a roller skating rink. The Bexhill Lecture Society met there. We used to go to the lectures in the evening. Father believed in educating his family.

We got our love of music from Mother's side of the family, the Taverners. We were taught to play the piano by a German teacher. She was Frau Von Hippius and she was quite a socialite. I remember reading in a copy of the *Bexhill Observer* or *Bexhill Chronicle* and seeing her name in the list of people who attended some sort of occasion. I think she was well born in Germany. She used to come to the house and sometimes I went to where she was staying, she had a room in Parkhurst Road on the right where a man named Burgess used to live. He had a grocer's or greengrocer's shop in Town Hall Square not far from the Bijou Cinema.

My brother Jack and I went one day to a foxhound meet outside the Sackville Hotel. At that time the Bexhill Golf Club was on both sides of the railway. On the south side it ran to the bottom of Galley Hill, on the north nearly to the Hastings Gasworks.

Paul Allan Hodgkinson and Jethro Arscott

I think there have been the most changes along the sea front. In those days there was little shingle on the beach especially opposite the Sackville Hotel and at the end of the promenade opposite Richmond Road; the sand came up almost to the sea wall and enterprising artists used to draw pictures in the sand of cathedrals and other large buildings at low tide. I remember the beach-huts had big wheels and horses took them down to the sea. The Colonnade was quite an important place at one time, built in 1910, we used to go

Paul Allan Hodgkinson in about 1921

down to concerts there. In fact I remember we had a Christmas party with quite a lot of children, we were taken down to some concert or amusement. It was all glassed in. I think they served teas there. There used to be a fortune teller near the right hand entrance. They had band concerts outside. I remember the bandstand outside the Kursaal. That would have been Herr Wurms and his White Viennese orchestra. That was when they had the gates onto the De La Warr Parade. I remember the motor racing, and I remember seeing a circus procession around the town and seeing the elephants being put on the trucks at the West Station.

We were not a very strict religious family, though we went to church regularly on Sunday. We started off where Father was a sidesman at St Peter's, we were all baptised there. When Father thought things were rather high church there we went to St Stephen's on the Down. After church Father took us to the Iron Well and we drank the water from a collapsible cup. I was prepared for confirmation at St Stephen's but this took place at St Barnabas where they held lots of confirmation classes. Occasionally Father took us to St Barnabas for Evensong. I sometimes went to the Presbyterian church where my Mother went. I was in the choir there.

Fire brigade practice was held at the Devonshire Hotel and people slid down shutes from the hotel bedrooms, I don't know who they were but I think I would have liked to have been one of them. It was great fun. When there was a fire the horses for the fire engine in Amherst Road, galloped down Station Road past our house on the corner, from their mews in Middlesex Road.

I left school at about 17 or 18 I suppose. I had no part-time work before that. I was an apprentice at Weekes, Tunbridge Wells and I think my wages were about five shillings a week. I travelled daily for the first year as I couldn't afford to look after myself. I was friendly with Henry Gibbs, whose father had a firm in Ashford and there was Len Cobb whose father had a furnishing firm in Margate and we were altogether in the same digs. As we were at Weekes we belonged to, and didn't have to pay the membership fee to the Tunbridge Wells Tennis Club. Our apprenticeship lasted about three years.

When I met Barry Lucas I became interested in the history of the area, particularly the iron workings. Barry used to work as a chemist at Boots; he was a member of the Sussex Archaeological Society and helped Ernest Straker in the compilation of *Wealden Iron*.

I remember a concert party on the lawns at the west end of Marina Court which stood at the east end of the De La Warr car park. There was another concert party in the Pergola in the Egerton Park, which is now the Indoor Bowling Pavilion. I remember seeing the Mikado at the Kursaal. I was a founder member of the Folkestone Operatic Society. In fact I took part for about seven years in nativity plays in Bexhill; I was Gabriel, I took two or three other parts and was once one of the Kings. We took the play to Ninfield and Hooe and to a church behind Kings Cross, London. Mrs Jacobs who lived in Watermill Lane, wife of Colonel Jacobs, was the leading light. I also took part in the Battle Abbey Pageant of 1932.

HARRY HALLS

Mr Halls was born in 1907. His mother ran a grocery and provisions shop in Windsor Road which sold everything from 'a pin to an elephant'. On leaving school he became an apprentice plumber and then worked in the building industry in Bexhill and elsewhere.

I haven't taken sugar in my tea since the 1914 War. We used to go blackberrying then to try and make a bit of jam, and we had to save our sugar; we couldn't afford it in tea. We used to have Newbury's jam from Battle in our shop. All these big firms in those days had travellers; we used to get travellers come round. We sold grocery and provisions; practically everything, from a pin to an elephant. We had a double-counter shop. That was a lovely shop [in Windsor Road].

We came here for my father's health in 1910. He developed TB. I was born at Catford, Lewisham. My father had three other brothers and three sisters - there were seven of them. Two of his brothers were ticket collectors at Waterloo, one on this line and one on the South Western terminus, and the other brother was at Deptford Water-works. Their father, my grandfather, I never knew him, was a main platelayer on the London Bridge section on the old South Eastern and Chatham Railway, and he was killed, pushing another man out of the way of the train.

Unfortunately, my father only lived 10 months after we got here. He died July 21st 1911 and was buried up here at Clinch Green on July 24th, which was the day the Colonnade was officially opened on the front. I was four and a half when he died. I wasn't allowed to go near him. I've only got one photo of him.

My mother had to do something so she took this shop. Her name was Mary, and it was her name over the shop. We rented it. We sold milk and paraffin, the paraffin was out the back. Everything came in bulk. Sugar was all in Hessian sacks, two hundredweight. Common washing soda was in Hessian sacks, and everything had to be weighed up in those days. Children used to come in with a basin for a pennyworth of jam, a pennyworth of syrup, a pennyworth of treacle. The vinegar used to be in barrels; Sarson's vinegar wasn't in bottles. Look at bananas, for instance - the price of them now - they

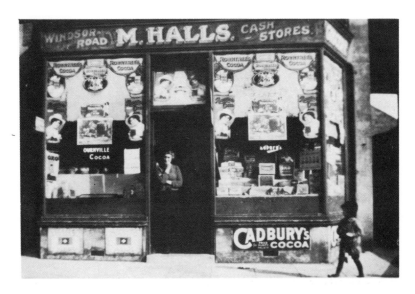

Mary Halls' shop in Windsor Road

go by the pound. In my young day, they went threepence a 'hand' a big bunch of bananas, more than five. Look at swedes; we sold bushels of swedes - a penny each - and now they go by the pound. People never got paid till after six o'clock Saturday night. My mother used to open her shop half past seven Saturday morning and she wouldn't close till one o'clock Sunday morning. There was just my mother and me, and my old grandmother - my mother's mother; she was with us.

Then of course, my mother was taken ill. I had to run from Windsor Road to the Albert Road surgery, when it was Doctor Murdoch's private residence, at one a.m. I had to blow through the speaking tube, which blew a whistle up in his bedroom. He answered and he came to my mother. She had heart trouble. You know the old iron bed on the castors - it was going to and fro. My old grandmother came to me crying; would I go and get the doctor. Well, I went and got him and he came. I said to him 'Is her heart bad?' He said, 'Well, it's got out of gear, she's been over doing it and she's got to have a rest.' I was about 11 then, I suppose.

My mother's sister - my aunt - lived in North Finchley, at Tally Ho Corner. I had to go up and get my aunt to come down to help my grandmother and me to look after the shop. I went up to the West Station for the train to Charing Cross, and went down on the Strand tube. In those days you could book right through to Tally Ho Corner. It was seven pence, and the Northern Line then only went to Golders Green. I had to get out at Golders Green and go on the Golders Green Road and get a tram back to North Finchley, to Birbeck Road where my aunt lived, and I had to bring her back. My mother got on all right. She lived to 86 and my aunt lived to 91 and my grandmother lived to 91. Pretty good, wasn't it?

When we came here, they couldn't keep me in, because of having the shop. There was stables, coach-houses, in Windsor Road called Preston Mews. The back door opened onto a yard; we had to go out into the wash-house place at the back to get all our water. My poor old dad used to come and try and find me. Then he used to go back and say, 'I can't go another step; I'm exhausted; I can't find him.' I was so young - of course, no garden - they couldn't keep me in. It was all horses and carts in those days. My mother never got the Old Age Pension and my father died before the National Health came in, in 1912, so she never got a penny.

I went to school to the Infants at the bottom of Western Road, what is now the Library. The Infants was in the bottom and the Girls was on the top. Then from there I went to the Boys which was in Reginald Road. I was about seven and left at 14. We had the 'Three Rs' and we had a little bit of geography and a little bit of history, and Friday morning we used to have a bit of religion. The Reverend Mortlock used to come from St Barnabas to take prayers about half to three quarters of an hour, with no teeth in! 'Caley' Poulton was headmaster - he lived in Station Road as it was then, not London Road.

In those days Station Road used to come from the Central Station across in front of the Town Hall. You didn't have to go right round like you do now. Station Road finished at the bottom of Belle Hill. From Belle Hill to where the council houses start in London Road now was North street. That is as far as it went. You couldn't get to Sidley that way. You either had to go to Barrack Road and up past where the Hospital is now or up over the Downs, down Gunters Lane and back along Turkey Road. London Road was built soon after the 1914-18 War.

Before I left school, there was three of us, Charlie Croft, Reg Standen and myself, we used to go up to the Central Station and get the papers. It wasn't electrified in those days. Hastings had their own London trains that used to go straight up through there, and didn't go into Eastbourne. Eastbourne had their own London trains; they went from Stone Cross straight through to Polegate. They've pulled the lines up now. We used to go up there [Bexhill Central Station] and used to have to carry the papers across the line and put them on the down platform, and used to load them on the railway trolley and run down that down platform and used to go out onto the old station. As you go into Sainsburys car park now - the old goods yard - there's a big tall brick wall. That's where the old station was behind there. This was the first station, and we used to come out through there and down to Westbrook's, which is White's now, in Town Hall square. After the Castle [Hotel] there used to be the Bijou which was a concert place before it was St George's Cinema, and then Westbrook's was the next shop.

In the local paper last week, there were four firemen in there, Pat Sweeny - the left hand one - Clem Burgess, Perce Scrase, Cyril Smith. They [Cyril Smith's family] came there in 1914 from Redhill, and they lived next door to us in Windsor Road. Their father was a shunter at the old West Station goods yard, and then he was signalman from the station. He was the last one to live. They had a garage in London Road opposite Cambridge Road. They've pulled it all down now and they're going to build a block of flats, so his nephew said- he put the piece in the paper about Cyril. He'd left some money to the Fire Brigade, because he was on the Fire Brigade looking after 'Lady Kitty'. That was his pride and joy. He was a fireman mechanic, so he was apprenticed in Russell's in London Road; Station Road, I want to keep calling it.

Russell's was only half the size it is now, and the other half was an open plot. We had a garden in there, and Mrs Sharp who lived in the house next to it - she owned all the property where we were, and the yard behind us. Then I worked for Mr Harm, where Austen's used to be. He had a garden there as well, and he used to keep poultry down Devonshire Road, in a big house that he had built. I remember vacant plots in Devonshire Road and St Leonard's Road, and front gardens in Western Road and vacant plots. Bexhill is nothing like it used to be. Miller and Franklin's had both sides [in St Leonard's Road] where the Unemployment is now, each corner of Wilton Road. Longley's have gone now. They were down in Devon-

St Leonards Road

shire Road. Old Mr Longley used to live in Sutherland Avenue, at a house called Westleigh; and that was the sons that came along later in St Leonard's Road and then took over Sabins when Sabins finished up. We put central heating in there about 1923 or 24, when I was apprenticed to plumbing.

When I left school, I used to go to Collington Stores of a morning to do papers. I used to have the afternoons off, and in the evening I used to go to Miss Field and take goods out for a friend of hers, a Miss Newton who had a haberdashery shop in Devonshire Road, next to Jensens. Mr Francis who started Collington Stores used to be the manager at Gammons in St Leonard's Road. Gammons had a provisions shop and grocers on the corner of Eversley Road, and Ward's - what's now in Devonshire Road - was on the opposite corner. Mr Francis left there about 1920 or 21, and went up and opened Collington Stores when there was only half of it built. I used to work there [at Miller and Franklin's in St Leonard's Road]. I used to work for Miss Field, who used to have a hat shop, ladies' hats, straw hats, millinery. That was halfway in between. There was a vacant plot there and then Gills was the hairdressers, then Miss

Field's, then came the chemist's which is a chemists today - Schofields - who lived in Broad Oak Lane. And then came the china shop of Miller and Franklin, and then the furnishing department, and then of course all the drapery was over the other side.

Terminus Road, now that's all built on. There used to be nothing on the left hand side from Sackville Arch right up to the Nursery which was opposite West Station, run by a man named Mr Corney. He was killed in the 1914 War, then a Mr Smith took over. Mrs Corney, the widow, lived in Colebrooke Road. All Colebrooke Road wasn't built on in those days. She was in the choir, which I was in from a boy of seven, at the Wesleyan Church in Sackville Road - corner of Parkhurst Road.

When I left Collington Stores, when I was 16 and a half, I went into plumbing. I had had enough of grocery and being indoors and that; and I used to go round for orders. I used to go out to Barnhorn Lane, when there was pieces cut out of the bank for horses and carts to pass, when you went over the old road over the marsh. In the old days of driving, it used to take you about half-an-hour to come over there in November when it was foggy. You couldn't see. You just imagine the carbide headlights. You had to have a running board and you had carboys on there and a red rubber tube running into the lamp, and all you got was oil lamps on your windscreen. In those days it was all cranking. Advance and retard used to be on the steering wheel, and you used to have a ring on the front that you could flood the old carburettor, and let go again. The first thing I drove was a Fiat lorry that had come out of the 14-18 War, and the handbrake and gear-lever were outside, and it was all double-declutch; no synchromesh gears in those days.

I served five years on Stranges in Terminus Road. They built a lot of property in Bexhill. They were good builders. Five years apprenticeship. The first year I had nothing, my mother was having to support me. The second year I had five shillings a week, the third year I had seven and six. This in old money of course, and the last two years, as improver, I had ten pence farthing an hour. I used to work eight to nine, two and half hours a day more in the summer than in winter. Easter was the worst holiday of the lot because they shut down from Maundy Thursday till Tuesday morning. That was half a weeks money gone, and you never got paid for it [a Bank Holiday] unless it came on a Sunday.

In those days, I used to go haying, at the side of Collington Woods. You know Collington Avenue; well, between Colebrooke Road and Westville Road there was no houses there. Terminus Avenue wasn't even built. Westville Road - there was only one house and then you went into a field. The next one up before you get to Sutherland Avenue wasn't made [Holmesdale Road]. Cranston Avenue wasn't made; it was only a track. There was two houses on the right going towards Sutherland Avenue, on the corner of Eastwood Road, Downlands Avenue and Downlands Close wasn't made. Out in the middle nearer to Eastwood Road was Offin's, the butchers slaughterhouse. Then you went over Sutherland Avenue. You never got houses until you got to Sutherland Avenue. There was one on each corner [of Cranston Ave], Stone House on the left going, and [on the right] the house they've pulled down and built flats on, Fearnan, that was called years ago. You went straight across to the other part of Cranston Avenue, and there was a house on the right about 40 yards up, and then a stile and a footpath right across to Collington Lane, to Collington Manor where Daniel Mayer lived. There was a pond. He owned Collington Woods in those days. All that property was his, all through there, Walton Park and all that. This man I used to go haying with, Mr Ashdown, who had the yard opposite us in Windsor Road, he looked after all that.

When I finished my plumbing and my apprenticeship, I had a month on the dole - ten shillings a week - and five shillings they kept back of the first week, 'cause you had that when you started work. Well, you wanted that when you were out of work, not when you went back. When you'd got your week's wages, you had to go back that night and see a man named Mr Boakes, to get that five shillings. I was a full-blown tradesman then. Things was bad then.

A friend I knew worked at Wordley's, the electrical people at Norman Road, St Leonard's, got me on there, and I was on there about five or six months. I helped them with various jobs, and then I had to go down the East Sussex Hospital to fix up. There was one of the lights in one of the operating theatres that was coming away from the concrete ceiling. It's a terrible job trying to get fixings in concrete, and we had to fix that thing again. Then we had to take the sunray treatment out, from this place underneath, as it was going to be put somewhere else.

Before I left there, I went with a man called Wally Mills, he wasn't married, out to near Batemans at Burwash. It was up on the hill, you go to the War Memorial and you turn by the church - I think it's called School Hill. Batemans is on your right and you go up to Brightling Needle. They'd built a big house there, and we put country house lighting in there. We'd a three horse petrol engine on a concrete bed, and we had 27 big glass cells, batteries, which we used to charge for lighting in the house, and a well 90 feet deep for this Petter engine. We had a shed built over it and a water container over the well, with an endless chain which had cups in it and used to go right down, and this Petter engine used to drive that, to bring the water up. We had to work until about eight o'clock at night. It was in November, and we used to lodge with an old lady named Mrs Thompson, behind the church. We didn't come home; there was no conveyance in those days. We used to come out of there of a night with a candle in a jam jar; after we had been working with the electric light, it was pitch black dark.

Then Mr Wordley's mother-in-law died, and, me being a plumber, he asked me to plumb the house in Clive Road. There was a basement and three stories, and I plumbed all that. When I'd finished, there was a water inspector came round, an old boy with a beard, and of course I'd given them the same as we had here, and given them a tap off the main for drinking water. He said, 'What's this?', I said, 'A tap for drinking water.' He said 'Where'd you come from?' I said 'Bexhill.' 'Ah,' he said 'you can't do that there 'ere! All our water has to come off a tank.' I said 'Off a tank? We're not so old fashioned as that in Bexhill. Why is it then?' He said, 'Well, we haven't got a constant supply at night. Our mains are so old; our water's shut off from ten o'clock at night until six o'clock next morning.' I said, 'What do you do when you've got a fire?' 'Well' he said, 'We have to have a turnkey on duty every night - in case there's a fire, he has to go and turn on.' That was Hastings in those days [1930s].

Then I went away. I hadn't got a job here, and they were advertising for plumbers, for Miskins, a firm at St Albans that were building 600 LCC [London County Council] houses at Yiewsley next to Uxbridge. So I thought, I think I'll have a go. So I went up on Friday and the foreman wasn't there, so I saw the second in charge. He said 'All right, well, come up Monday and start.' So away I go Monday morning first thing - with two bags of tools When I got there, I saw the foreman. They put me on my own, doing what we call 'second fixing', fixing up lavatories and that, fixing the high level cisterns on the wall. After I'd been there a day or two, this foreman came along and he said to me, 'How you getting on?' 'All right.' 'Yes I can see that.' We got talking, and then I said, 'I've seen you somewhere.' He said, 'Have you? I don't think so. Where do you come from?' 'Bexhill.' He laughed. I said 'You've worked down there, haven't you?' 'Yes, I have.' I said, 'Now don't tell me. When we were building Stoneways Mansions at the bottom of Devonshire Road, you worked on Sainsburys that was being built, didn't you?' That was a vacant plot. He said 'Yes you've got it.' Now wasn't that funny that I should run into him.

Well I'd been there a month and I was getting fed up. I wanted to get back to Bexhill. There was four of us in one big room in Yiewsley. So I came home. I thought I'd chance getting a job, and was asked if I would play football for Bexhill. And so I did, and this is how I came to go on the Gas. The superintendent of the Gas Company in those days was Mr Bexley, when he retired, he went back to live at East Grinstead, he was a supporter of Bexhill playing at the Polegrove then. I played with them against Haywards Heath, when Harry Parks and Bert Wensley and Jimmy Parks, the old Sussex cricketers were playing for Haywards Heath, and Haywards Heath had a pretty good team. Well, I scored the hat trick that day against them. I played centre forward, and Harry Parks said to me 'You can move, can't you? It takes me all my time to keep up with you.' Harry Parks was considered one of the fastest outfields in County Cricket. He finished up working for Johnny Carter at Hastings, who couldn't read nor write.

I got married in the Wesleyan Church in Sackville Road in 1933, half past nine Christmas morning. Even Vielers, the well-known photographers in Station Road opened their studios for us, on Christmas morning. My wife was Winifred Fellows. All her family came from Brede. She had a lot of relations who moved down round Ashford way, in Kent - a lot of cousins - but she didn't know them. She also had a lot of cousins in this town. She was three years younger than me.

DAISEY SPANDLEY

Adopted when 18 months old, Mrs Spanley was brought up by a family owning a nursery and small holding in Amherst Road.

I was born on 10 March 1909 in Haddocks Hill, Bexhill, all Wrestwood Road now. My father was a groom and my mother a ladies maid. My father and mother didn't want children and I was chucked out. I was never told anything about my real family and relations, as far as I know I haven't got any. When I was 18 months old I was adopted and taken to the nurseries in Amherst Road. Mrs Wood, that's who had the nurseries then.

Then there were five fully stocked greenhouses and we had a field on the other side of the road where we growed fruit veg and kept chicken. There was plenty doing then and I loved the work. The greenhouses were on the present site - at the top of Amherst Road - but the houses on the other end of London Road that was an orchard and the entrance of Amherst Road was then in Belle Hill. But I don't remember that - it was before my time. That land was eventually sold and those houses built. It makes the house look as if it is sideways on to the top of Amherst Road, with now a derelict field and some remains of one or two greenhouses. [They] recently received planning permission for a block of flats, so it has been dug up. It was a nice house with two sitting rooms, kitchen and scullery and a nice big cellar.

We grew flowers, fruit and veg and we had chicken and all kinds of bedding plants and crysanths - early ones and Christmas ones and we made wreaths. The only thing I didn't like was the holly wreaths, if you have to do 200 it makes your hands all raw all the time you'd finished wiring that holly with the prickles, but I used to love all that work.

I went to St Peters School in Barrack Road. It is still there, but the council houses that are along there were all allotments in those days. I left school when I was 14 in 1923. I had a short spell at Eversheds in London Road, on millinery. It's now called the Pop In, next door to the Salvation Army. But after a time it was thought I should do better doing housework and I was put on to housework in between working in the nursery. I was always kept busy.

95

I was five when the First World War broke out. It was nothing like the second, no bombing, apart from having the Canadian soldiers here. The soldiers came to the nursery sometimes, for a bit of salad. If they had a girlfriend they'd come for a bunch of flowers. That sort of thing. They were friendly, over friendly some of them, if you know what I mean.

I was never left free. For a time I had three jobs and it got too much. I suffered from anaemia and bad circulation, I was always on iron. When I was four they had me working - they were over working me and the doctor said I should go to school to get away. I went and thought this was lovely - no work to do, but when I got home it was all saved up for me. In the garden, feed the chicken, pick fruit according to season, pricking out, watering, when tomatoes were coming along, whatever job there was to be done. There was a son who helped. It was only through the season we had a girl come in and an old chap to dig. But in the winter we had nobody.

My parents worked, mother did particularly as my father worked for the coal merchant Adams up in Sidley. So it was muggins who got left with most of it. Some of the family was interested. When they all went down to the beach for the day, I hated the beach, and from five onwards I could be left to look after the nurseries and serve the customers. I knew how to serve them and what to charge. The list was put out for me and I'd prefer working in the greenhouses to going down to the beach. I didn't like the sea. The greenhouses were heated by coal fires, coke. I used to take a candle in a jam jar and take the dog. There were three boilers, before and I went down to fill them up and clean them out so they lasted till the morning. Till I was 30. The boilers were done away with and in the Second World War the greenhouses were badly damaged. They had a direct hit next door where Mephams is, the furniture people. That was smashed to pieces, greenhouses were weakened, old house itself was all right, it is about 250 years old. It was built by a Mr Russell from Old Town so we were told. I don't remember who had it before. When I was 18 months old my foster mother took over, she died there. Then the son-in-law took over and then he died and the grandson took over. Been put up to sale but building plans weren't passed, now I think they are.

My maiden name was Rolfe and I lived at the nurseries until I was 26 and then I married in 1936 and became Spandley and lived at 232

London Road, just above Sedgewick Road. We had one son. My husband was a Ninfield man. He was at one time a milkman and he used to come and deliver the milk. Then he went into Western Road, fruit and veg shop, then moved to Gardner's newspaper, Surridge and Dawson. In 1940 he was called up and in Germany when the war finished. He had odd jobs and helped at nurseries. My husband was a heavy smoker and he died when he was 48 - heart lungs and liver gave out.

I only had ten shillings as a widow, and when it went over to old age pension it was still ten shillings. Things must be better now. It's more expensive but we can do things we couldn't do in those days. Then you were tied down because you worked long hours and no one had any money or transport. The Poppies was our only pleasure, cause it was sixpence and the pictures were one and nine. We had the Ritz where telephone exchange is and Gaiety bombed.

For entertainment there was the Kursaal down the bottom of Sea Road, on the beach, near where the sailing club is. They moved into the Park Pavilion. The entertainment they gave, for sixpence or nine pence a high class show, you wouldn't get it anywhere now. They damn well worked hard. They lived here, mostly local people and the enthusiasm. You never came out of there after two hours without feeling right on top of the world. I thought they were marvellous. Mind you, we didn't have television in those days. The park was still there but the Polegrove was just a bit of wasteland and they put all the rubbish there. Town rubbish and it built it up and then turned it into a sports ground. We remember the De La Warr - they took down the coastguards' cottages above the colonnade. Then five steps with this monument with a drinking fountain. They built the De La Warr the other way, parallel.

IVY FULLER

Mrs Fullers's account illustrates the village-like character of Sidley earlier this century and provides glimpses of being a child and then working as a young woman in the family grocer's shop.
Ivy Fuller was born in 1909.

My father came to Bexhill in 1913. He had a grocer's shop in Sidley Street and then the 1914 war broke out. And I can remember my father going off one morning on his bicycle wearing a Norfolk jacket. It had a pocket at the top and he filled that top pocket with golden soveriegns to go off to the wholesalers which was at St Leonards, Stuarts the grocer's wholesalers, to buy up food, as much as he could, to stock the shop because he wondered what the war was going to bring.

Then during those years the men were called up into the forces. We had friends at Little Common, grocers also, by the name of Elliot, and the sons went. Mr Elliot was an invalid and he managed, sort of, the shop from upstairs. But his sons were called up and of course the staff was difficult to get. So my parents and myself as a small girl, on his bicycle, we went over to Little Common to help weigh up the stock for the shop so that the people in the shop could serve. They used to do that after our own shop was closed at night. The Elliot's shop then was more or less up the Twitten at Little Common. Well now at the moment there's a hairdressers there.

Also in Little Common I can remember that there was the village green, not where the roundabout is, but somewhere about there. Then there was the little chapel that was connected with the Methodist Church at Bexhill and that was where there is a new terrace of shops laying back from Meads Road. But they were cottages along there and a little chapel was there.

When we used to go to Bexhill when I was a child we used to go to the station and then cut through the fields until we joined London Road. From Sidley we used to walk to Bexhill through the fields and joined it where the Malet Hall now is. There's several older type of houses either side of the London Road and that was when we were in Bexhill. Otherwise it was all fields through there.

Our own shop was at seven Sidley Street, on the corner of Sidley

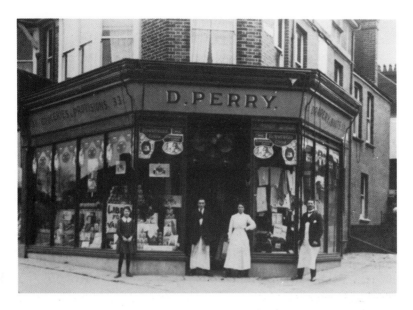

The Perry's grocery shop, Sidley Street, 1917

Street and North Road. Next to us was a butcher's and next to that was another little shop and the next one was used as a church, a little Meeting House, for many years. I can remember going there to Sunday School. Then after a few years there was Haddon Hall, which was a tin hut built further up Sidley Street on the left. It is now Sidley Baptist Church but of course it is all altered. My father was Superintendent at that Sunday School for years.

Well then after a while my father moved down into the corner shop where it is now Sidley Post Office, big premises. Perry was my maiden name. Our provision hand was Jack Marchant. That was before the Post Office came over here. Father took his business over there, then after a few years the Post Office which used to be down the road came here. Wickens had it. Their grocer's shop was just beyond the Sussex Hotel on the right hand side. Wicken's and then it was Dobson's. We lived over the shop. That used to be boots and drapery and on the ceiling of the shop was all hooks, and on those hooks was all household things, brushes and pans and things like that. And then from this side going along in the shop inside was all large containers for the food that you would have loose, sort of flour and tea. That was in tubs, behind that was the great tubs. When my father sold the business, he sold it to some people called Wickersham.

We worked very late at night at the shop. I think father used to be open till eight at night and the Post Office closed about seven. Course Saturday nights were later still for the shop. A person used to come in and do the cleaning in the house, cos my mother used to work in the shop as well. Mother did the cooking. Between the house and the garage there was a concrete entrance and I remember the washing used to be hung up on lines across.

I came home from school to work in the office. We had two assistants and also the telegram boy. They used to deliver the goods, but also we did telegrams there. When the telegram came through he had to put his belt on with the telegram in it and go and deliver it round the area. We had a telephone in the shop and they would ring there you see. There was quite a big delivery area of Sidley, and they did the delivery from there. The provision hands used to wear the aprons and the jackets in those days. Father's car was a Morris Oxford. Our garage at the back was big enough for four cars. It was a stores and over the top was also a stores. In that was also a place where you could develop films in the corner, black room.

As a child I can remember taking, my friends and we'd go up the stairs into there and we'd have a wonderful time playing up in this store room. It was quite a big building, we had the upstairs and the downstairs. The dining room was behind the shop. My parents bedroom was here, another bedroom here. And my bedroom was around the corner, there was a double window and my bedroom was sort of joining on to the shop next door. And there were also two very large rooms right at the top, two bedrooms.

My first proper school was the infants school at Sidley which was along by Sidley Church. Oh it was very small. I can remember the little forms, two together you sat at a desk. Mrs Kimber was the mistress there and her son married Betty Westington and she was Councillor Mrs Kimber. I went from the infant school to the school in Barrack Road. We used to walk through the little cutting at the back of Sylvester Road and go to school there. And I also can remember that at that school, 'cos it was Church of England, we used to go to church, in a crocodile from Barrack Road up to St Peter's.

I was an only child till I was twelve and then my brother arrived which was quite a space of time wasn't it? In those years I used to go to Lewes Secondary School. We used to walk from Sidley to Bexhill Station and then we went up by train. There was quite a group of us that went in my age group. We used to get on the train at Bexhill and we went straight to Polegate. Now at the moment the train goes into Eastbourne, but then the line went straight through to Polegate. And on the train used to be the boys that went to the schools in Eastbourne. They got off at Polegate, and invariably they had got one of our top hats. We had a uniform with a little hat and of course a gym slip and so on. We went up to Lewes because there wasn't a secondary school here. Some of the other children went to private schools, but this was the Lewes Secondary School for Girls. We did that for four years. Except for the time I had an accident which resulted in having a bone removed from my arm. That took about four years out of my education. After I came out of hospital I was allowed to go up to school with my arm in a sling so that is why my education is not perfect. I started at Lewes at twelve.

Well then I can remember Old Town, when I used to go to school. I can remember the Manor grounds, now you can go into it, but there was a big wall where they had the horses and that in there. And right in the centre, [where] now you go along up Chantry Lane and up to Old Town, I can remember that there was a few shops there. There was the post office which you had to go up steps to it. I think it was somewhere about where the doctor's used to be. And there was a grocer's shop on the corner and a baker's right opposite and Schindler's, the jewellers. And right in the middle of the road there was the tree.

Then there were also times when we used to go to Hastings. We used to walk up from Sidley up the cut to get from Chantry Lane to the church. We could walk up past the church and round into De La Warr Road which of course was quite different from what it is now. There were trams and we used to walk so far to De La Warr Road to the fare stage. That used to be about where there is a nursing home now. We had to be careful with the money in those days and we used to be most upset because we had to walk all the way to the fare stage. Then it used to go over the fields at Glyne Gap, and it used to wobble and wobble, you know.

Well of course my parents were very religious and we used to mostly be entertained in the church by going to meetings. I must tell you this little bit about the drapery. My parents used to go up to

The Walnut tree, Bexhill Old Town

London to buy stuff from Thomas Cooks at St Paul's. I remember going up with them, I loved going up, used to go up every so often. I would get a new outfit, they would buy a new outfit. I used to be most annoyed because they'd show it in the shop first and take orders from it afterwards.

There was only three shops. My father's big shop on the corner, next door was Slade's the confectioners, and then Well's the boot shop. I can remember that when my father bought this property, it was quite a big property, he was offered these other two shops, the whole lot. I think for six hundred pounds. In those days my mother was very careful, and of course it would mean taking out a mortgage and so on, and she didn't want anything to happen. But the thing that was most against it was that Slade's, the tobacconist and confectioner, used to open on Sunday. So she didn't want to have anything to do with people who did that. But further along the road here there used to be a wheelwright's where they did the hammering. I can remember spending hours in that wheelwright's place. I loved watching them, the sparks flying up from the anvil. It was a proper place for children. They would watch there for ages.

Just this side of the forge, I can remember the first buses that went from Sidley to Bexhill, Carter and Lidstone's. They were buses which had the long seats down either side as you got in that way. It was quite an event to go down to Bexhill on the bus. There is a triangle in Sidley and it used to stop just this side of the forge. Then also I can remember the trains ran from Sidley to Bexhill. Now at the present moment it is a garage, but that was Sidley Station right opposite the Pelham. The station master was Mr Sands. I remember going to school with his daughter. But the gentleman who was more or less the porter and general factotum was Mr Mockett. It used to be a great event to go down to the station and go on a train to Bexhill West. Now it is the garage and auction Rooms. When we went to London we used to go down to the station and the train went up to Crowhurst via the viaduct.

My father was a councillor, he put up for the council in 1930. That's Councillor Perry, my father. He was also a very wonderful first aid man and they used to call him the doctor of Sidley. I've got the clock that was presented to him by people when they left Sidley.

The shop, October 1930

We had a lady who ran the post office in the shop. She lived in with us, she had one of these top rooms. Her mother was taken ill and she had to leave to go and look after her. I'd always wanted to do the post office, so [at] half term my mother came up to Lewes and asked if I could be released. I was going to leave at the end of the term. I remember coming home and taking over the office, of course with my father's help in the shop, and putting my hair up. I was sixteen. I was in the office until the time I got married. In those days one could have your driving licence without any test, when you were sixteen. I had my driving licence at sixteen and my father put up for council and I can remember the very day my licence came through I was driving that car and picking up people to take them to the poll. I was Miss Perry then!

Sometimes we used to come down to Bexhill and where the indoor bowls pavilion is in Egerton Park. It was much smaller then. There was a little place where there was a concert party and the stage of the concert became part of the Egerton Park bowls. I believe it was called the 'Poppies'. We used to sit on iron seats, folding seats with slats across. They were hard and the floor was small pebbles. I can also remember going down to the Kursaal. Right opposite the Kursaal was then the Glynde Hotel, now flats. We used to come down to Sackville Road Church where they had organ recitals. Miss Wimshurst was the organist. Harry Foster was there and also Miss Wimshurst's brother [who] had the chemist's shop which is now Boots. He was a councillor. I can remember Longleys. It started off first as a tiny shop in Devonshire Road.

We used to go to the band in Egerton Park. There used to be a bandstand right in the centre of the lawns there. There were chairs all round. They used to have entertainment. In the summer time they used to have the Children's Special Service Mission on the beach. We used to attend that where they had meetings and entertainment for children. Then on the Colonade we used to have the bands and the orchestras. We came there quite a lot to hear the bands. My father used to go swimming quite a lot, but I was always scared of the water. We used to come down to the Egerton Park swimming baths from the school.

I was paid a pittance for my job because my father used to give me so much a week. I think I had the enormous sum of two shillings a week pocket money and my parents clothed me. As I got on I was very upset about this because it wasn't the clothes that I wanted. So I kept on at father that I wanted to be able to clothe myself so he increased it to four shillings a week, and then I had to buy my own clothes out of that. It was very difficult of course so I grumbled more. It sounds very bad but I grumbled terribly and I wanted more money. We used to get an allowance for the telegram boy and the sub-postmaster was paid so much for each delivery however far it went. So after my grumbling about it my father said 'all right then, when I'm paid the delivery money for the telegrams you can have that money.' So I used to be very pleased when we had lots of telegrams.

In Sidley I can remember Pankhurst Mill and that was through Sidley, Mayo Lane went up that way and Pankhurst Mill was on a little bit higher. There was a small incline to get to it, and the mill was standing at the top there. I remember going there to see the workings of the mill. It was still a working mill when we were there. I can also remember Hoad's Mill at Gunter's Lane. The Hoads used to bake cakes there quite a bit.

There were several farms round Sidley. There was Buckholt Farm. At the side of the New Inn there was a pond and houses there. Then we used to go round the side of that and down the Lane to Buckholt Farm but of course there's all houses now.

From the Sunday school we used to go just past Pankhurst Mill off the Ninfield Road, down there was a sort of wood and playing field and we went there for our Sunday school treats. We were taken in carts to this place and I can remember father taking all sweets and things that we could buy. And he made a stall up there. We had races, many races. It was a great event to have all these bits of tables fitted up and we had a good feed and that.

I can always remember the opening of the De La Warr Pavilion. My father was a councillor and he and my mother of course had an invitation. They went to this grand opening when the Duke and Duchess of York came down. It was a wonderful occasion. And Earl De La Warr, I think, was there.

My father used to go preaching in all the villages. We used to go to Ninfield and Boreham Street and Herstmonceux. We used to cycle in those days. I remember on one occasion we were going out cycling, down Standard Hill and I fell off my bicycle and I went into a traction engine that was there. That was when we were going preaching. My father was sometimes asked to take Sunday school anniversaries. And there was a young fellow from Icklesham came into the shop one day to ask my father if he would go to Icklesham to take the Sunday school anniversary. Now thats the other side of Hastings, you know, just before you get to Winchelsea. Evidently it was a case of yes he would. I saw this young fellow, you see, quite nice, came up on a motor bike. Frank Fuller, his people had a market garden out there. And this was the young fellow I married eventually.

HARRY FOSTER

Both Mr Foster's parents were members of the Salvation Army. His father was a poor cobbler with a shop under living accommodation in Windsor Road. He also describes working for a Bexhill estate agent between the wars.

I was born in Bexhill in May 1909 when its population was about 14,000. My birthplace was in Windsor Road where I lived for many years with my parents and brother, eight and a half years my senior. My father was born in Rye and when he came to Bexhill he worked for C. Wells, a boot and shoe repairer and leather dealer. Subsequently my father opened his own small business, a rented shop, in about 1898, in Terminus Road next door to what was then a temperence hotel on the corner of Windsor Road and Terminus Road, facing Sackville Arch to the South. He then moved to my birth place in Windsor Road comprising a shop and living accommodation. My mother had lived in East London and her father, who was a policeman, moved his family to Bexhill because of unsavoury happenings in that area of London. My father was still a cobbler and so remained all his life. And, apart from shoe-repairing, he occasionally made footwear to fit deformed feet.

My mother was a member of the Bexhill Sisterhood, an organisation which met weekly, I seem to remember at the Victoria Hall, and their interest included the visits of speakers from time to time. One of its facilities enabled members, if desired, to pay a fund whereby one was included in a doctors panel. My mother enrolled me at birth, I understand, for only one penny a week, and the doctors attendance was otherwise free. The medic was Dr McCulloch and his visits were by bicycle.

My brother worked in my fathers business and we were extremely poor, not withstanding the fact that none of us drank, smoked or gambled. My father had a 10 rod allotment in Terminus Road and my mother did charring and occasionally let a room to balance the books. Windsor Road and almost all the houses in the town centre and those in the Honies (that's Cambridge, Havelock, Beaconsfield Roads etcetera) London Road and many in Sidley were constructed towards the end of the nineteenth century, but some in

107

Foster's boot and show repairers

the Old Town, much earlier. In fact apart from updating, these areas have changed very little in my life time, although there were still some private houses in Western Road. All the small terrace houses were built without a bathroom and most if not all had an indoor WC.

My parents were both members of the local Salvation Army Corps. My father was in the band, was bandmaster at one stage; my brother also was in the band. My mother sang. On Sunday, it meant that about 10 o'clock, or soon after, they would join what they called an open air meeting in one or two roads of the town until 11 o'clock when they would go to their Citadel or Hall. It used to be in a top room in Windsor Road, but later on it was in London Road where it still is. In the afternoon they would go to another open air meeting which, in the summer, would be on the West Beach, near the Clock Tower. And then in the evening they had an early service, sometimes outside, and then to the hall again. So one can say that, apart from meals, the whole of their Sunday was occupied by their attendance at the Salvation Army outside or inside. I used to attend in my earlier days Salvation Army Sunday School.

Apart from that, my father, as I mentioned, had an allottment. It was very, very heavy clay soil and very hard work keeping it going and so it took a lot of time. He was helped by my brother I think. Later I had come into the picture, which I didn't enjoy very much.

My mother was quite a good singer. I wouldn't say she sparkled as a solo singer, but she was pretty good and she had a relation who I think was in the professional class as a singer. Her time was taken up at various meetings.

I do not recollect my parents ever going away on holiday although they may have gone away for a day or two here and there. My father would sometimes go with the boot and shoe organisation on a trip to Tunbridge Wells or somewhere like that. My father was quite a keen member of the Tunbridge Wells Equitable Friendly Society and that served my family extremely well, because we had various benefits from it.

I was five years old when I became a pupil at St Barnabas Infant School which is now the Public Library. As a matter of interest, some 37 years later I negotiated the sale of that building, which for part of the Second World War was a furniture depository, to the East Sussex County Council, for use as a Public Library. I wore shorts and continued to wear shorts when I started work. Mr Jethro Ascott, the father of Ascott the solicitor, who had a very wonderful business in Western Road, bakers, confectioners and restaurant, said to me, isn't it about time you were in long trousers?

The school was within three minutes walk of where I lived. Being so close to the school I came home for lunch, and so did all the boys as far as I can remember. The Headmistress was Miss Roberts, a charming lady. And I remember one particular dissertation, talking to the school, or perhaps it was just the class I was in, about living the good life and receiving rewards for living that sort of life. It always stuck in my memory rather. Another small incident was that I'd never seen anyone faint before, but once when I was sitting at my desk next to Froggy French he fainted and I was quite startled. It must have been 12 or 15 years later I would see him driving around the town and the country, with a milk conveyance, drawn by a horse, with big churns on it. I never heard that he fainted when he was driving. He was a frail sort of chap but that was, of course, quite a heavy job he was then doing. I quite well remember standing at the corner of the building, corner of Western Road and Sackville Road,

109

ringing the assembly bell. Those days, the school was enclosed by a fence. Upstairs were the senior girls and I never remember seeing a girl there.

I was 14 when I started work at an estate agents which was on the 23rd July 1923. My hours were a quarter to nine til one o'clock and quarter past two to six o'clock, sometimes half past six and sometimes seven. My duties were to sweep off the front where dogs had sometimes been, to sweep down all the offices; to dust them; if it was the winter, to make the boiler fire, to keep it stoked all day. Then at about 10 o'clock having done all those chores. I would clean up and then be ready to do some office work. The office duties included delivering letters, either walking or sometimes on my bicycle, and copying letters by some antiquated system and a very different one in some ways because one copied the typed letters, and there were also letters written by copying ink and it was very difficult to put these through the copier and not smudge.

In those days we had a typist. She was a Miss Mildred Cruise, who came from Battle daily by train. Her father was the Battle Abbey Agent. Miss Cruise was a most efficient typist and interviewer, highly intelligent and to the best of my recollection she earned one pound, eleven shillings and sixpence a week. I should think she was about 22 or 23, course she seemed a lot older to me as I was so young.

Then I began to be sent out to accompany people looking at places. Those days there were houses, flats and maisonettes to let as well for sale. Actually we had quite a big collection of weekly rents, which I used to do later on, for someone like a Mrs Holden, who owned quite a few of the houses in the Honies. But they weren't the sort of thing one showed, so much as perhaps maisonettes over shops; over the Maypole in Devonshire Road, maisonettes in Sea Road; and those sort of places. Some people lived over shops, although not when they were company shops so much. Some did, but I can remember we used to have a very fine maisonette over what was Hudson Brothers, in St Leonards Road. That was a first class grocer's shop and that was a very good maisonette with five bedrooms and two reception rooms. Of course we also had quite a fair business in letting furnished accommodation. People used to rent houses furnished, for a month as a minimum, sometimes three months, sometimes a year. And a number of people took these houses were people home from abroad for long vacation.

Harry Foster (right) and friend

I began to do quite a lot of this showing people round, and I remember them saying to me at the office in the early stages, if they ever offer you a tip you take it. And did I not! I did extremely well with tips, thank you very much. When someone wanted to look around we did go in their car when they had one. We had no office car and in [one] particular case the man was going on his bike, so what could I do but get on my bike and accompany him.

In letting houses on no account would anyone be given a key, one always had to accompany. That was laid down very firmly. That meant going out quite a bit with those sort of people. A four bedroom house with a garage in Cooden Drive would have let for for 12 or perhaps nearer 15 guineas a week in the prime month of August. And then of course, I began to interview people. We also let beach huts on the East Beach and the West Beach. Huts were let for a month and six weeks at three guineas a week. Some people took the hut right through the season. The agent got 10 per cent for letting and collecting the rent which was quite a worthwhile occupation. One occassion we let a hut to some people, subsequently they returned to us and said they wanted to buy a house. We sold them a house in Brassey Road, a 10 bedroom private house, after having let this beach hut. That was a wonderful bit of business.

Generally speaking it was local people we let or sold to, and such a variety of people. There was a few of the artisan type. Not many, but in Bexhill we then had quite a number of people coming here in retirement and buying houses. And there were people who bought houses to run as apartments or guest houses such as Albany Road, Albert Road and Wilton Road.

One of the interesting places was Channel View on the sea front to the left of Devonshire Road. One day I was asked to show a gentleman, Mr F J Harris, down to look at number seven Channel View. He suddenly appeared on the scene in Bexhill in the late twenties. I'd never seen him before. He was with a lady. Took him down there and the lady. In number seven was a lady who rented this place on lease and she wanted to assign her lease, and so he looked at it and, very polite, spoke to the lady and to me. And it must have been some three or four weeks after that, my govenor, Mr Sheather, heard that this Mr Harris had bought the whole of that terrace, 12 places, through another agent. He was very upset about this, although of course we hadn't got them to sell anyway.

Well, Mr Harris apparently bought these from the Webb Estate. It was this man's way of looking at one no doubt. Channel View was quite different than it is now, because they were each let individually. There were 11 of them plus number 10A, a little place on its own, in which there was a boiler which heated all the lot. In those days the lower part was rather basement and a pretty horrible part of it too. There was one room down there which was obviously the servants room. Ghastly place! Mr Harris then proceeded to improve them. He spent about £900 on each of them, which was a lot of money then. Subsequently he put them on the market for about £2,850. It's only since the war that most of them have been converted into two flats, which I think in a way is a great shame.

In 1926 of course we had the miners strike and they were out the best part of the year, and for a short period, I believe seven days, we had the General Strike. Business round about that time was very bad indeed. But the General Strike had no great impact on a place like Bexhill such as it would in a city. The General Strike was only a week, so it didn't affect rent collecting. The collection of rents covered a wide area, including parts of Sidley. I used to toil up to the top of Galley Hill every fortnight either by shanks pony or bike, collecting the six shillings a week rent.

When the strike was over, I can remember the acclamation in the office. Well in fact the tenant upstairs came down and complained about the noise. What happened then was that in America things were becoming very bad indeed, and when America sneezes we got pneumonia here, and business continued to be pretty awful. I can remember having as many as 300 places on the books at times. It was very sparse particulars we handed out then. I could reel off these particulars of these places without reference to the book, typing them out because one was doing it, all the time. There must have been weeks when we didn't sell anything, but we did have other things in the office. We collected rents; we managed property; inventories for furnished letting; insurance agents; building society agents. The office was agent, and later became branch office, for the Hastings Permanent Building Society.

When the Labour Exchange was in London Road I saw queues of men down there. They were local people who were unemployed and the unemployment situation [was bad] because building had quietened down. There was a big building boom at the end of the

Harry Foster when a young man

century.

Because I wasn't all that fit I couldn't indulge in some of the social activities that some of the boys and young men did. But when I was at school I had played cricket and football. I was in the football team once or twice and I ran a boys club in Sackville Road Methodist Church before the second world war. And we had a cricket team in that club and I played with them sometimes. Apart from that I played tennis at Egerton Park. We used to do a bit of bathing in the sea. A lot of people bathed in those days. In fact the club had quite a big hut on the beach. I started playing golf before the war started at Bexhill Club which was at the end of the De La Warr Parade. And my friend and I joined the Artisan Section. We'd only been in it for about six months and the war came, and subsequently the golf course was mined when invasion was feared.

I was in one or two other organisations, the Red Cross, and one of my big joys was singing in choirs at Sackville Road Methodist Choir then later on the Bexhill Chorus. I had a fair voice those days and used to help out other choirs sometimes at special occasions. I was very keen on that.

I never remember going with my family down on the beach, ever. I don't think I was unique, but you've got to remember that the whole of my father's day was taken up by work. Either in the shop or on the allotment, or in the Salvation Army.

I was never a keen cinema goer. I hardly went. As a matter of fact, of course, the cinema was frowned on by the Salvation Army, but that didn't deter me going when I wanted to go, later on. But I never was mad on the cinema with one or two exceptions of things that I did see. 'Love on the Dole' for instance at the time, the terrible times, that did something to me. In the late twenties [and] early thirties there were four cinemas. There was the St George's earlier called the Bijou in London Road, that's just in Town Hall Square; there was another one down near the York pub that was called the Gaiety; there was the Playhouse in Western Road; and for a short time there was a big one in Buckhurst Road where the telephone exchange is now. That was a skating rink before it was a cinema.

What we also had then was the Kursaal. That was built by Lord De La Warr. It looked like a short pier rather. When I began to know something about it was in the time when it was run by the Pavilion Company and it was managed by Fred Pepper, who was the brother of a more well known Pepper, Harry Pepper. I've been in that place when they've had professional variety shows and not 50 people there. It was getting pretty awful, and then suddenly Philip Yorke and his Barnstormers were invited. They came to the Pavilion, and took off. It put Bexhill right on the map for repertory. Later on Mathew Players used to perform year after year at the De La Warr Pavilion, others too, but that was the sort of repertory in Bexhill.

The Kursaal was a German sounding name and they dropped that during the First World War and it became the Pavilion. By 1935 the Pavilion Company wasn't doing at all well and they wanted to sell it. The Pavilion Company then let off part of the area of the beach, on it's west side where the Sailing Club now is, to a firm that made a leisure centre of it. A noisy, brash centre with dodgem cars ecetera, right in the heart of this town. Bexhill couldn't take that and of course they had to buy it. They paid a heavy price for it. Having bought the Kursaal it was pulled down, and so the De La Warr followed on from that.

When the First World War started I was five. I went to school soon after the war [began]. There was a lot of sadness there because one of the tradesmen opposite had a working horse, and the military just came along and commandered the horse. As a boy I had some pretty good idea that horses were being killed in their thousands in the fields of Flanders, and I can remember now the hush in that shop, never shall forget it. The Canadians were stationed here. That was just up my street! They used to get into what they called squads in Sackville Road and there'd be a squad drilling and then they would sing 'Oh my! what a rotten singer too!', and you'd hear that. One day at the junction of Wickham Avenue and Woodville Road, I'd been watching them and I could do their drills too, and they started showering me with pennies. I didn't mind at all! I must've gone home feeling good.

I remember my mother having the ration of margarine. You used to get it from the Maypole in Devonshire Road. It wasn't enough, so she bought some other ingredient to mix with it.

During the First World War a large area of land, now the South Cliff and north of that area, was occupied by troops as a training area. Live ammunition was used, and after the war one or two boys, perhaps more, handled live grenades and suffered injury.

While I was still at St Barnabas Boys School, it was 11th November

1918, another boy said to me - his name was Coombes - have you heard there's an armistice? I wondered afterwards how he got to hear that, there was no wireless in those days. It was only recently that I heard when the armistice was declared it was announced by the Mayor of Bexhill from the steps of the Town Hall.

BERT KIFF

*Born in 1911, Mr kiff graphically describes his Bexhill childhood and
talks about the development of Sidley in the inter-war years.*

My mother was a Catsfield girl, Naomi Stubberfield, and my father
was a Chief Petty Officer, Royal Navy. They were married at
Catsfield Church on Christmas Day 1910 and moved to Newington,
which was between my father's bases at Chatham and Sheerness.
We lost dad on New years Day 1915, when HMS Formidable was
lost. My mother found work in the orchards to help supplement her
pension and in October 1915 we moved to our grandparents in
Silvester Road, Bexhill

For a few months I knew Bexhill Old Town as our local shops.
Starting with the Behive sweet shop, then Pococks the butcher, the
post office, Waite and Whybourn Dairy, and Cave Austin the
groceries. On the opposite corner to Cave Austin was a jeweller and
blacksmith with the old walnut tree in the centre of the road. Doctor
Kent was in Dorset House.

In mid 1916 we moved to rooms at 20 North Road [Sidley] and
later in the year took over the whole house. Our furniture, which had
been in store was delivered by horse drawn van and number 20, now
number 30, became our family home. My brother still owns it today.

I was sent to All Saints School, aged four, and the headmistress,
a Miss Berdette, lived in the School House. The staff was one other
lady teacher, but after a year Mrs Kimber came from Norman's Bay,
lived in School House with her family, and the school sort of came
to life. Mrs Kimber treated all our cuts, also did our throats with
iodine and pulled loose teeth. Later a school nurse took over all these
things. At the age of eight I moved to St Peters Boys at the bottom of
Holliers Hill [now a row of cottages]. Mr Bunting was the headmaster, our form master was Mr Waight. I spent some happy years there,
playing football and cricket for the school and was picked out as a
future player by Mr Waight.

North Road was only partly built up and an allotment made up
much of the road until the second war prefabs. At the bottom of
North Road was a boggy swamp at the rear of the New Inn and the
path around this led to the main road, but there was a short cut

around the back of Mrs Eagling's house, between the house and Beal's forge.

The main street at the time started at Wickens which was the post office and general stores, with two thatched cottages between the shop and the Sussex Hotel. The landlord was Mr Buxton, later Councillor Buxton, after whom Buxton Drive was named. Above the Sussex were more cottages, then Arscotts the bakers. On the north side of the road was Beals the engineers and also the forge, then Mr Tom Bodle's house (he owned the farm where Burnt House is and Bodle Crescent), above which were empty shops and a space which later became Barnett's the chemists.

Turning up the corner to Sidley Street were several empty shops then Mrs Franklins store, Pococks the butcher and Mr Verny on the corner of Suffolk Road. Opposite, on corner of Suffolk and Sidley Street, was Mrs Burton, the paper shop. In Ninfield Road north side, was Mr Green the sweet shop, where our first penny ice-creams came from. Opposite on the south side of Ninfield Road was Livingston House, then cottages which had long gardens running down to the road. Joining these was Mrs Sinden's black board Cottage. This lady was midwife and helper to whole of Sidley.

Passing on we came to Adam's Coal Yard with the brickyard behind, and the footpath ran from here up to Hoad's Mill. I was in the mill during its working years, also at Pankhurst up Ninfield Road. At the other side of the footpath were eight small cottages attached to the brickyard. Then Adam's house and All Saints School, with the Institute and All Saints Church and Vicarage. On the opposite side of road was Sidley House which employed quite a staff of gardeners. From there on apart from Arncliffe Terrace, Turkey Road was a country lane. With the building of the Grammar School the road began to develop.

When Wicken's finished Mr Dobson built a new shop, but the post office was taken over by Mr Perry who moved from the Suffolk Road corner shop to the large shop at bottom of Sidley Street. This then became a general stores and post office, which remains the post office to this day. Also up Ninfield Road was a small enclosure of elm trees with iron railings which became known as 'The Irons' to all us children. Opposite was Turners the blacksmith and wheelwright, now part of the DIY stores. Just below was Sidley Working Mens Club, part of the original Mission Hall. Above Turners were Lewes

Lass Cottages, still there and just opposite Beals wheelwright works.

When you used to leave Sidley station there was a muddy footpath which went down right down through to St Georges Road where St Georges junction is. That was a metalled road from then on. That applied for a good many years. There were buildings, there were houses, but not so many, but they gradually came, and gradually filled in other parts of Bexhill which were all fields. We gradually saw the erosion of lots of open fields. Glenleigh Park was one of our best mushroom fields. It was called the Mill Field in those days, and where the council houses are now, Southlands, that was open parkland, all lovely open parkland, but that was all filled in. Then the era came where they started filling in every little space there was to fill in Bexhill. Its gradually grown and grown and it's almost built up now.

Generally speaking as far as Sidley was concerned we knew everybody and everybody knew us. But now we know nobody. It's different. One of the differences of course in the Sidley area they were all rented houses, and now they are nearly all self owned.

When I was eight years old I joined the All Saints choir under a lady organist, who carried on until Claude Young returned from the war. In the early days the choir robed in the Institute and on wet days made one dash across to the vestry. Father Ellam was the popular parish priest. A bequest from Mr Aitcheson of Preston House led to the finishing of the church, and I remember watching the East window being constructed and assembled on the floor of the Institute.

With the finished church the choir had a fine vestry. I had become a server after my voice broke and had the honour of serving to the man who started the church in Sidley, Father Wigan. We had a fine Boys' Club going thanks to Father Powell, he bought equipment and we had a football and cricket club.

I must mention that as war orphans we were treated to all sorts of shows as free treats. The Playhouse, St George's and the Bexhill Players are some I remember. Also a great treat in my school days at St Peters Boys was the trip to the Wembley Exhibition. The only choir outing I can remember we choir boys went to Firle, where the Reverend Ellam had transferred to, and we played the Firle boys at cricket. I made my first 50 and we beat them by a few runs. The only other outings we got were from Claud Young, the choir master. Now he would take us to shows. Where the telephone exchange is in Buckhurst Road there was the Winter Gardens and quite a lot of shows were put on there. Well usually once in the winter he would take all us boys to this show. Also on firework night he would also give us a good firework display.

We played a game called 'Tibby Cat' which seems to have died out. It consisted of a four inch stick sharpened at each end, the stroker stood in a circle and hit the 'Tibby' as far as possible, he then had to tap the pointed end of the 'Tibby' and hit as far as possible then pace out how far one had gone from the circle. The winner being the furthest distance from the base. It was [also] a recognised thing to go to the blacksmiths, and you had an iron hoop made to suit you, and then you had a stick with a nail in it and you pressed that along and you could run this hoop where ever you liked. Some had a hook, but I always had a stick with a nail. You ran miles with these things, just for the sheer joy of it, through Sidley and around the woods anywhere round here. I took mine right out round Buckholt. Places where you never expect to see one. But we enjoyed ourselves.

We always had a joint on Sundays. And one of my favourites was to go to the Institute on Monday to pay the coal and clothing club which was run by the verger of the church, a Mr Baker. He always sat in the Institute door and took the money on Mondays. And I used to rush home from school on a Monday, rush into the larder with a knife, dig the dripping, get the lovely loose dripping at the bottom and, even if it was pork dripping, I used to have a good go and then run before I was too late, cause he closed at five, and pay our money in. I always remember my grandfather saying to me 'One of these days my boy you'll quod yourself.' Which is an old Sussex word, meaning you'll sicken yourself. And sure enough he was right, the day came when I got my dripping, ran to the Institute with the money and I didn't run back. I was sick and I had the most awful bilious attack. And I have not touched dripping from that day to this.

We always had enough to eat. It was Sussex pudding, suet pudding, vegetables and gravy. We had our own little allotment. Puddings were usually jam roly polys and that sort of thing, cause it was the war years and food was short. And I can remember, we had to collect our margarine ration from the Maypole or The Home and Colonial next door, half way down Devonshire Road, somewhere where the Arcade is now. And I went with my aunt, we walked from Sidley and we formed up round the other side of the Devonshire [Hotel] in the queue and we got, by slow degrees, right across St Leonards Road and down to the shop; and just when it was our turn, I will always remember it, he opened the door, and said 'That's all for today.' So we went all the way back to Sidley without any margarine. It wasn't a very big ration; but my aunt went back next day and got it. But it meant going with your ration book once a week to get it.

When I joined the Athletic Club in 1928 the club room was in Amherst Road behind the fire station, just a room over an auction room of Burstow and Hewett. At a club dinner in the Devonshire Hotel, Reg Cane, a founder member suggested a fund was started for a new club building, and after several years the club house in Little Common Road was built. The Club did not use it until after the war, as it was taken over for ARP [Air Raid Precaution] use. The Club also ran a weekend camp in the Highwoods with a small swimming pool which attracted many of the members.

This pool started as a small spring with a small basin so you could wash your feet, gradually a bath was introduced. And someone suggested we dig the clay out, and we dug quite a big piece out, and there was a nice overflow. That spring never failed and so that pool was always full with an overflow running down into the woods. The only drawback to it was, being in clay you stirred up mud and the

'A Sunshine Group', Highwoods Camp, 1934

first one in was lovely 'Rickett Blue' but after that it was real muddy. Well, I can't think who the benefactor was but somebody paid for the pool to be properly concreted, with a handrail round it. I don't think it got used as much after that lovely work had been carried out as it was the old mud pool, the membership seemed to have fallen away. But its gone now of course, its been filled in, it was dangerous to animals.

My mother wanted me to join the swimming club, because I was going to sea and I couldn't swim and the Egerton Bath was there and I learnt. The swimming club used the old Egerton Bath and had a very strong water polo team who won the Sussex Cup on two occasions. Gala nights were held and it was a job to find standing room, with somebody at the door at the top of Egerton Road taking the money as you went in. These were grand nights, these gala nights because other clubs came from away and joined in competitions and races and that sort of thing. All this was in the early 1930s. I had already purchased a boat, and I kept it at Normans Bay and I went to sea from Normans Bay. From there I eventually came and joined the Bexhill Angling Club.

At the age of 18 I joined the Bexhill St Barnabas Football Club and played for them until 1935, when after six years of being the best junior side from Bexhill and with many league and cup successes, I left to join Bexhill Town. I had been secretary for five years, but left on a point of principle. I played County League football for the Town Club when we were the only club south of Lewes in the County League and many of the West Sussex clubs did not like the long journey to Bexhill. Our aim in my time was to stay in the League and avoid having to apply for re-election. We played on the Downs. Some of the junior matches were played on the top pitch on the Downs. They built a small pavilion and we had a nice little ground there. In later years, when I was playing for Bexhill Town, we played in the Polegrove, with much better facilities for washing and cleaning after the match. In the early days it meant you went home grubby because there were no water facilities or anything to wash.

The last game I played for Bexhill was against Hastings at the Pilot Field when they were playing Southern Amateur League. We played them in the final of the Freeman Thomas Shield and we lost three-two, unfortunately. We were playing a man short all the second half. Three down at half-time, we made it three-two with 10 men, which

Bexhill Swimming Club members on the beach in front of the club hut, West Parade

with a bit of luck we could have won or drawn anyway, but we didn't and that was the end of it.

The Polegrove as it is now was an entirely different kettle of fish to what it was in those early days. When I first remember it, it was a black mass where all rubbish was tipped and then in-filled and covered in to make into a recreation ground . During the last war it was ploughed up and cultivated. Its developed some very nasty bulges in it, which is a pity. At one time it had a football stand at the North end which was built of timber, and one Saturday afternoon when I was down there watching, and my cycle was stored at the rear of it, the excitement got so great, suddenly the stand collapsed. I don't think anybody was seriously injured, but I was lucky, my bike wasn't either.

The other place that I remember as a tip was Turkey brickyard. And all the refuse was collected by horse and cart in those days. And you see lines of horses and carts going along to Turkey brickyard at various hours of the day to the tip and in-fill and that was completely in-filled. There's no sign of it today. It was rat infested, and if you could turn up the correct *Bexhill Observer* it records somebody seeing a great army of rats going up through the Highwoods, leaving the brickyard. He was on his bike and he just kept going. I remember reading that in the *Observer*.

I was apprenticed as a carpenter and joiner to Messrs Cave and Brookes. One of my first jobs was converting the old farm buildings just in Ellerslie Lane into the Highwoods Golf Club. We also converted the barn at the end of Highwoods into the Forest Barn. Cave and Brookes was in Devonshire Square, somewhere where the Bexhill Building Society is today and the works were, just below Chepbourne Road in London Road and round back towards the goods yard. The timber yard, the plumbers, the bricklayers, the painters were all housed in that establishment. Later they built a new workshop, which is still there today, at the bottom of Springfield Road on a rough piece of ground which they owned. A tile company own it now. Originally it was planned for another storey. It's built so that another storey could be added to it. It's all cavity work, and nine inch joists so that you could go up with another storey, but that never took place. Also permission was granted for two cottages in front facing Springfield Road and a garage at the end. The garage was built at the end, but the cottages never materialised.

QUEENIE JEWHURST

In this account Queenie Jewhurst remembers her family and home life, and many of the people and places and everyday events in Bexhill earlier this century.

I was born thirteenth January 1911 in St Leonards Road next door to Hampdens. We had a baker's and confectioner's business there when I was born. It is now the estate agents. Unfortunately I was the only child. Mother would have liked a large family. My mother had very bad thrombosis after I was born and she used to say we met along the Promenade, I in my pram and her in her bath chair for about six months.

I did have my cousins Doris and Sid. My father and his brother were partners. My grandfather started the business. Father was born in one of those little row of cottages, little two-storied houses, all joined along Ninfield Road. They are painted pink now and are almost on the road, but when father was alive there was quite a decent sized garden. All the family came from Sussex.

We didn't stay in St Leonards Road terribly long. My aunt, Doris and Sid's mother, was very ill when she had Doris, she nearly died. Doris was only three pounds. They never thought she would live, but my grandmother took her in hand. She was born in 1910, I was born in 1911 and Sid was born at the end of 1911. Their father was unfortunately killed in the First War, so father became their guardian. When aunty was ill she was looking after the Windsor Road shop and she wasn't strong enough to continue. So we went to Windsor Road and mother looked after that shop. It's now the vet's and the chiropodist. Of course the bakery is still there behind, but that is now Barnes and Watsons, printers.

I had very good parents and I wasn't really an only child because when my uncle was killed we all went over to Reginald Road to live. We had two houses and my aunt and her son and daughter lived in one and my parents and I lived in the other. So I was always with them. My cousin Christine who was born in 1911 and also went to Mountcroft lived with us during World War One. We had a door knocked through so it was like one big house. The garden was all in one. Then my aunt took them out to America when I was seventeen.

Queenie Jewhurst and her parents

Queenie aged two

But my cousin Ernie came down to learn the trade and he was there till he got married. He pinched my friend, her parents were Hoads, the oil merchants who had a business at the bottom of Windsor Road.

My first school was Mountcroft in Parkhurst Road. I think most of the town's business people's children went there. There were the Toziers, they were Swiss. They were at the top on the corner where it is now a bank; Eric and Geoffrey Sewell who owned the Devonshire Hotel; Leslie Heather, his father was manager of Hall and Co; Edie and Gladys Sheather, they were related to the milk people; Margery Davis, her mother had a gown shop and her father a saddler's business in Devonshire Road. The school was not very big.

There were seniors and juniors. We had two rooms [which] used to be split. There were curtains went along. I never smell disinfectant, very strong carbolic, but I think of these curtains. They must have been soaked in it. Of course we all had slates. It was quite good fun. They used to push the desks back for us to do exercises, as far as I remember we did them every day. Seniors had the best room with a nice, big bay. Its flats now I think, on the corner of Albany Road. I went there until I was about ten.

Then of course there was nowhere to go in Bexhill, no grammar school. My father and his brother and I suppose quite a number of other business people had to say they would send their children to the grammar school to get it built. But then the war came and I was 16 when it was eventually opened. So quite a number of us went to Wellington College in Wellington Square, Hastings, if we were not bright enough to go to Eastbourne or Hastings or Rye grammar schools. The three Warburton girls went to Wellington. I was the youngest, they used to bully me. Our headmistresses were Scottish and at the beginning of the war, 1940, they were evacuated from there and the school just broke up. They were too old really to start again. There is a memorial in the church in Hastings to Miss Bathgate. Joyce Perrett, she was another one, whose father was a chemist in Devonshire Road. She still lives in Amherst Road now, she's seven years my senior.

We learnt dancing over at Wellington with Mrs Russell whose nephew owned Russell's Garage. She used to teach us ballroom dancing, and we used to learn the positions of ballet, that sort of thing. We were also in a display in the theatre in Hastings. She had all her various pupils there because we were just an offshoot at the college you see. She did all kinds of nationalities dancing. We were Japanese. My cousin Doris was in a plough dance, she had to have a smock and everything.

Uniforms at Mountcroft was just green and white bands round our straw hats and a badge, on our pockets of our blazers and green tammy shanters in the winter. But Wellington was black, black bands round our Panamas and a metal badge, gold and orange. And we had to wear grey and yellow blouses under our gym tunics. It was a horrible colour. We went by train. The station had been altered then and we had to run up the hill. Mr Holden, the station master, used to open the gate for us at the bottom, very often. We always

Pageant celebrating the incorporation of Bexhill, Queenie Jewhurst is on the extreme right

used to wish it [the station entrance] was still at the bottom in Devonshire Square.

I think I missed the train once when I fell down and had to go home to have my knee bandaged up. Unfortunately I'm allergic to heat and skin trouble developed so I had to leave there. I spent my fourteenth birthday in the Buchanan Hospital. It was just on my hands and feet and they were putting hot fermentations on, which is one of the worst things to do actually. I had to go up and down to London after that. Then we went to Clark's College so we still went by train. That was over to Brighton every day. It wasn't too bad going to Hastings but going to Brighton it was quite a long way. Then after that I used to go three nights a week studying catering and cakery at the technical school, that was a bit exhausting after doing a day's work.

On Sundays we went to church, mostly to Sunday school cos we were Methodists. Funny, Mr Arscott [another baker], he was Methodist too but they used to go to Sackville Road and we used to go to

Belle Hill. Mr Thompson [also a Methodist] who we amalgamated with after the First World War had his bakery in Town Hall Square and we were in Windsor Road, but we had a much bigger bakery and grounds than he had.

We always had horses right up to the Second World War and then we gave them up because one of them bolted. The horses were called up in World War One. I think it broke my father's heart because they came round and took the horses. They had a pool for the bakers, they sort of pooled their facilities, you see each one helped the other. Rations were short and Mr Thompson was called up. Well my father had polio when he was quite young and he was slightly shorter in one leg than the other, so he was left behind. We made the bread and Mr Thompson's sister-in-law, she was a great character, she looked more like a man than a woman, she used to do the confectionery over in their bakery - the little bit you could do in those days. When Mr Thompson came back they decided we would amalgamate and carry on.

We had animals all the time. My father used to rent the land [that's now the Trading Estate] from the railway, We had pigs and cows and chickens down there during the war. It is behind Reginald Road and there used to be a footpath down there under the railway arch and through an iron gate and through some allotments that were let out to railway men. I should think there must have been a couple of acres there. Doris and Sid's cousin, Alf, was a signalman and all the men used to wave to us when they went in with the trains. It was great fun really. We used to go hay-making there, and had parties. It was all fields up to where Cranston Avenue is and there was a kiss gate - you came out of an arch and through the iron gate where we went to the field, then you continued on and there was a kiss gate. Of course the general public was allowed on this land and I know we used to play cricket and that with the other children. There's Downlands Road there you see and there was a corporation yard and a funny little bungalow place back in there. Then there was a squatter's cottage on the Downs too, with a hedge all round and this little cottage in the middle. In Barrack Road there were no houses at the end at all, and we used to walk from there right over to Crowhurst through the fields and back in a day. We used to walk over to Cooden too.

My uncle was father's youngest brother, he went out to Canada, a whole lot of friends went out together. That was before the First World War and he and the Greeds went. My mother's younger brother, my uncle, he is nearly a hundred now. I think he is the only one left. My uncle and the Greeds came back. Then he and the two Greed brothers started building. It was Greed and Jewhurst originally. I think they built the first houses up on West Cliff [now South Cliff]. Of course it was all open then just like Galley Hill is. We used to walk over there. The Canadians were all camping there.

Unfortunately this aunt brought ringworm over with her and she gave it to all us children. Course we were thrilled with her, she was Norwegian, she was lovely and we used to fight to sit on her lap. Her boy, my cousin Walter, had had it but it had cleared up, and apparently she had taken it and it had developed on the boat back from Canada. She used to put her arms around us. I had two on my neck, and Sid and Doris had them in their heads. Well we couldn't go to school for about six weeks or more and that's when we used to do a whole lot of walking. We used to get plenty of blackberries down at the field. There was a sort of drive In at the back of our field and the people there they had pigs at the back there too. They used to bring our coke round years ago 'cos the bakery was coke fuelled. I don't suppose there was all that number worked for us in the early days, but we ended up with fifty working for the bakery.

Bank holidays my father used to hire a carriage to take my grandmother out in the country. I must have been under seven at the time. We used to go on Sunday school treats, because my father was one of the leading lights at the church. We used to go to Pevensey Bay and Norman's Bay by train and be down at the beach all the time. We used to wear these great paddling drawers, like navy blue school bloomers, horrible huge things! My aunt Annie made our bathing costumes. My mother and my cousin's elder sister had them alike, and we had little miniatures of these. Mother's had these skirts. How on earth they did any swimming! I don't think they did much. My father never came with us, he never had time. But he taught us to swim on a seat out in the back garden. We used to go to the Swimming Pool in Egerton Park. I got cramp in the deep end and nearly drowned once. We used to go in as long as it was open, I think that was November. We used to know Mr Wise, the father of Fireman Wise who was killed, that used to be in attendance down there. We were very friendly with him, nice old boy.

Course we used to go to the Colonnade to listen to Hilda Bor's and Rosie Paikin's Band. Hilda Bor used to come to Mountcroft School and she used to conduct the band. She was the daughter of the junior partner of the band. She used to come to Mountcroft too, and they used to push the forms all back and they used to do the ballet for us, Swan Lake. She was marvellous this girl. She used to play on the radio to start with quite a lot and conduct her father's band in the Colonnade, a great attraction, cos she was only about my age, ten or eleven. We used to go down, take a book, have a deckchair. You could get in for about sixpence, I think. They had some military bands in the summer too. Then there were The Poppies. We used to go down there practically every Saturday, they were very good. Tissington used to run them. Then they had the Lawn but that wasn't such high class. The Kursaal used to run a Concert Party, but I don't think we went there a great deal.

Actually Bexhill hasn't changed to that extent really except that they've pulled down all the nice houses, where Dr Stokes and that lived, and then we were so much more right in the country really. This field out here, my field, was all open space. Barrack Road stretched right across where the council houses are, and we moved to Barrack Road because we liked the view! There were no Buxton Drive council houses then, it was all open country. At the end of Barrack Road that was open country too. The only part of London Road that was a road was where those first houses are up to Edinburgh Road. Then there was a footpath through to Sidley Station, so you could go over the fields to Sidley.

We used to go out to Glover's Farm. It was just behind the New Inn. It was a lovely old farm. When I smell apples now - they had a room there with all the apples stored on the floor. We used to be allowed to take as many as we could eat. I also saw ferrets there for the first time. Shoesmith's the butchers had a farm, where the oast houses are down Watermill Lane. Course it was not made into a house in those days. We used to go there, and I was taken to the slaughter house where I saw a pig being killed. It put me off you know. The lane joins up with Watermill Lane, Freezeland's Farm, Freezeland Lane. It goes from Ninfield Road down to Watermill Lane. I've an idea that the slaughter house is still there. It was a brick one but it was quite a way from the actual farm.

We used to play tennis too with the Warburtons. They had a

house just at the bottom of Chepbourne Road which has been pulled down. It had a big garden and a tennis court. Also, a bit later on, my father bought some land from Mr Arscott which had a tennis court on. It was in St Andrew's Road, we always used to go up there after school. There was just this one bungalow next to ours which was Mr Wimshurst the chemist. Boots were next door to Wimshurst in Devonshire Road, and they took them over.

There were lots of schools. We used to serve St John's, we were always afraid we were going to lose them to Arscott's. My aunt Kate worked for us and she had unfortunately had an accident when she was young and she was deformed. That Miss Hamilton from St John's School used to make her go out and take the order from her in the car. There used to be 'toot toot' and it didn't matter what my aunt was doing, she had to drop it and go out to her. They were marvellous customers but very autocratic. When my aunt was laid up a couple of times and I'd started in the business, I used to have to go out there, I used to hate it. St John's was where Thrift House is at Collington Avenue. They were beautiful houses there, it was a shame they pulled them down. I think they were designed by Mr Maynard. His business was on the corner of Terminus and Collington.

I think he designed one of the extensions to our bakery at the rear of Windsor Road. My uncle, Greeds, they built the first extension onto the old bakery, and then Godwins built the final extension which was a two storey building. I think we moved to Barrack Road when I was twenty-one. We bought a house there. There are about six groups of semi-detached houses there. We bought one of those because it got a nice long garden. We bought it because of the view and the garden, not so much the house. During the Second War we had a lovely view of the gunfire and that, it used to be like a firework display.

In the First World War I can remember my cousin and I being right at the top of my aunt's house to look at a German plane. My parents were horrified afterwards. That was in Sackville Road. My uncle had a bicycle business there and they used to hire out bath chairs. I had a bath chair when I had this skin disease when I came home. They let me out of hospital for Christmas. My cousin Sid used to let me run all down the Downs, he was terrible. It was made of wicker. A friend of mine said when he first came to Bexhill the promenade was all full of old ladies and bath chairs.

When we were in Windsor Road we had the Fire Chief lived next door to us, Mr Wise. His nephew's statue is in the cemetery. I remember him being killed when he fell off the ladder at the Miller and Franklin's fire, the big drapers on the corner of Wilton Road. His father was a seaman and they used to live in a little house at the back of where there were three shops at the top of Windsor Road. He and his house keeper lived there.

We had a fire in our kitchen. We had a copper and the part next to it was all blocked in with boards and a lot of dirt and stuff had apparently accumulated there. Mother had the copper going one day and started a fire there. There was smoke all coming out. It was great excitement! We had what I think they called it a duck oven there. It was a most peculiar thing. You sort of pulled the bits round and put over the top, it was more like an open grate as far as I can remember. But we didn't see it of course until we had this fire and then it was all pulled out because they didn't want it to occur again. It had been boarded up you see and nobody knew what was behind there.

Jewhurst Bakery cart. Uncle Sid at horse's head, Uncle Bill at rear

I remember the night of Arscott's fire, my father and mother went. The fire was in their bakery in St Leonards Road, it was where there is a ladies dress shop shop now and a carpet shop. They had a beautiful cafe. Anyway twice they were burnt down and we made bread for them until they managed to get going again. We never had a fire at our own bakeries. The great excitement was the horses with the fire engines. It was the sound, we always used to know when it was a fire because a bell used to ring at Mr Wise's. Then of course there was a fire rocket went up and everybody ran, they sort of downed tools whatever they were doing. He was a plasterer and decorator. But it was amazing how quickly they turned out, in about two minutes they were there, dashing along, putting their helmets on. He had a lovely brass one and the others had silver ones as far as I remember.

Lady Brassey was to do with the Red Cross and we went out there to have tea with her one time. My two friends and I used to go horse riding all round there. We used to go to a gentleman who had stables at the top of the hill which comes into Ninfield and go all around Herstmonceux Castle and Normanhurst where the Brasseys lived. That was later, in between the two World Wars. We always used to put our horses out. They were kept in Leapold Road to start with, and then we had stables at the back of Amherst Road which I sold a little while ago. Its been taken over by motors now. Sid and I used to ride the horses down to the field, which father rented from the railway, to put them out to grass. Every weekend they used to go down there, we used to ride them bareback. Then I did have a saddle when one of them was saddled up. Because father owned Thorn Farm for a short time, that's the one with the oast houses. Only he had it at a bad time, he lost so much money, he decided it would be better if he got out.

One thing we used to like to do was watching the horses being shod. There was one forge up here on the corner. I think my cousins, Doris and Syd's, grandfather (he was a blacksmith) had it originally. Then he was Corporation blacksmith, and we used to go round into the corporation yard [behind the Town Hall]. Then of course there was one at the end of our road. We used to get hung up there on our way from school because going to Mountcroft up Parkhurst Road we used to have to pass it. Doris used to be sent back to see where we'd got to when we were late for tea.

We had a croquet set and used to play croquet on the back lawn in Reginald Road. I remember putting on my cousin Sid's trousers and dressing up because we were about the same size and going out into Reginald Road. When we came back in my mother said, 'You mustn't do that, you'll get summonsed for masquerading as a male!' Course we had hoops and scooters. And during the War the craze was to have a tin lid on a piece of string and run that up and down the pavement. It made an awful racket! I wasn't really allowed to play in the street. We were sent off down to the field. My father made us a go-cart thing. It was supposed to be for the goat but I don't think we ever got the goat into it. We had a goat and two kids. We used to go all day and make a camp fire and stew. There's a house there still, one of the fellows who used to work for us, his mother and father used to live in that.

There was great excitement at the building of the De La Warr Pavilion. My friend lived in one of the Coastguard cottages. Her father lost a leg in the war and they couldn't get anywhere to live. Being ex-Navy, he was given one of these Coastguard cottages. We used to go down there to parties. They were where the Pavilion is now, next to where what we called the Lawn was. It had just a stage with a canvas back to it, deck chairs round for the concert party. The Coastguard cottages were two up and two down. I don't think they had any bathrooms. The stairs went straight up from the lounge you know, just like a little bandbox. We used to have marvellous parties there all the same. There were still working Coastguards in the other cottages and there was a boat house down there where where the boys have their rowing club.

TOM PRATT

Born 1912, Mr Pratt joined Bexhill Fire Brigade as a messenger boy when he was 14. He tells the fascinating and sometimes breath-taking, sometimes amusing, story of fire-fighting in the town in the nineteen twenties and thirties.

At the funeral of fireman Sydney Albert Wise the whole street, Wickham Avenue, right along to where the traffic lights is was lined with firemen, us and other Sussex brigades. Everyone remembers the Miller and Franklin fire. Well the size of the building, you see, it was just unfortunate that although it was a very bad fire, what I think lives on in everyone's memory was the fact that somebody was killed at that fire. You know its a question of life against property.

I left Bexhill the day after the De La Warr was opened. I went up to Outer London in the Fulham fire brigade. Then it was bombed actually and I moved over to Epsom which was developing very much at this time.

Looking at this photograph of the Opening of the De La Warr Pavilion there is Mr Hoad on one side of the step. I was on the other, we were both in exactly the same uniform. You can't see me there 'cos they cut me out. I don't know whether you was down there two, three years ago, when they had the new stone laid, when the Earl came down. He said, 'It would be interesting to know if there's any people in the audience here tonight that was here at the opening ceremony.' I think four of us popped our hands up. One was Mr Dicks, whose father kept a blacksmith's shop at Little Common and myself and two others.

I joined the fire brigade as a messenger boy in 1926. I was 14. There was a vacancy then because the chappie before me, the other messenger, had just retired and well he was about 18 or 19 then. There were 20 members in the brigade. 12 of them were on bells. Now one must remember that was in the infancy of electricity and everyone had to live about a half mile from the fire station. One or two were just over the border. And these bells in the houses were rung one o'clock every day to be tested and they were operated between 11 o'clock at night and six o'clock in the morning.

Prior to the bells there was a maroon that was always fired 24

138

Opening of the De La Warr Pavilion, December 1935. Left to right: the Duchess of York (later Queen Elizabeth), Earl De La Warr, Lady De La Warr, the mayor of Bexhill (Colonel O Striedinger), the Hon. Mrs Geoffrey Bowlby, the Duke of York (later King George VI), the Mayoress and Mr R W Hoad

hours a day, but there were so many complaints about it they decided to go over to a house bell system between the hours of darkness. There were 12 men on the bells and we, the two messen-

The funeral of Fireman Wise, 27 September 1924

gers, were responsible for going out at night and arousing the other members out of bed. So I was living in the bottom of Windsor Road then, now I had a house bell. Prior to my house bell being fitted my uncle, who lived opposite, as soon as his bell went in the middle of the night [and] as soon as he came out of his house, he had to go straight over the road to rouse me. And my bike was always ready to take off straight away. I used to go then down under Sackville Arch, up Park Road and call two chappies out there, and from there I had to go along Egerton Road to the Coastguard Cottages where the De La Warr now stands and call out another chappie by the name of Scrace. His son replaced me as a messenger boy. Then back down Sackville Road, call one chap out there, then back to the fire station.

If the fire was fairly local then it was my duty to go on to the fire to see if they wanted any more help. Or some chaps hadn't got all their equipment, you know, and I had to go and fetch that to the fire. Somebody's boots or somebody's coat. The first machine out was the life-saving, the escape-carrying appliance and the idea was to get that onto the job as soon as possible. You didn't wait for an officer. Now the drivers were in a slightly different category to the firemen. They were drivers/engineers in those days and we had five or six drivers so providing you had a driver and a crew of four, that's fine, you went straight off. The senior man took charge.

Funnily enough 'cos I was only just eighteen at the time, I'd just been promoted up to fireman. Two or three new members had joined so although they were older than me, I was senior to those. And we got a call to the New Inn at Sidley so I looked round, 'One, two, three, four, five.' So off we went! And when we got there it was a rather nasty chimney fire. Well of course they can be a little awkward in such old buildings as that, but no more other officers came on the job at all. I phoned back to the station from the New Inn to tell them what we got and they said, 'Are you quite happy?' and I said,' Yes.' 'What have you done?' 'Well so and so and so and so.' 'Well that's all right, I wont bother to come up.'

And that was it. That was my first blood as somebody in charge of a job. But my first fire as a messenger boy was about five o'clock on a Sunday morning. So once I'd got the chappies all out, and I got back to the station the second officer said, 'Well it's number two Sutherland Avenue, Tom. You'd better go up on your bike and see the Skipper and see if there's anything you can do or what he wants.'

When I got there they got the fire out and under control. There was a very lucky escape really because the fire started in a rather large lounge/dining room. And I think one of the younger persons there had been a very active athlete at one of the colleges, Oxford or Cambridge, and there had been a beautiful show-case at one end of the room with all these trophies in it. The heat was so intense that the floor had all burned through and all these trophies had just melted into silver balls laying in amongst the ashes. The people had made a miraculous escape by running down a conservatory roof at the back and jumping down into the garden. Then they kept running up and down the street blowing a police whistle to attract and waken other people and they summoned the brigade. It was quite an experience! I always remember Jim Stevens took me up to the lady of the house, which was somebody possibly, and said, 'This is this young man's first fire.'

I served under Captain Stevens. In fact when he was seriously ill, just before he died in Bexhill Hospital here, I happened to come down for a week-end. And my other friend, he's still alive, he's 83 now and lives in Folkestone, and we both went to see him in hospital and I said to him, 'Well history is being made here to-day Jim, isn't it?.' 'Why is this then Tom?' I said, 'Well all three of us here started as call [messenger] boys.' He started as a call boy. I started as a call boy and the chappie that was with me, his father was chief of Hawkhurst brigade out in Kent, he was call boy one time of Hawkhurst brigade.

The maroon was very effective in a town like Bexhill, but you could only have a brigade summoned by maroon where there was no lifeboat. You see now Hastings couldn't be summoned by maroons because of the lifeboat. All the calls came through to the Town Hall Keeper and he, if he was at home, or his wife, took the calls. Whoever was available fired the maroon. Now he used to keep so many upstairs and out of the way, but he always kept one under the back entrance to the Town Hall in a tin box and just on that passageway there where there's a concrete pillar erected with the tube inside and the cap on the top. I don't know if you've actually seen the shape of a maroon but its like a peg top. Well the explosive part of the maroon is in this top and this top was all composed of cardboard and string glued together and then in the cone-shaped piece at the bottom, which was dropped down into the mortar, the fuse came out. That was the explosive charge that sent the maroon up into the air.

Now we, as I say, living all in a close range to a fire station, might be sitting talking or listening to the 'cat's whisker' radio, as it was in those days and all of a sudden you heard 'Whoom'. And you were gone. The time that burst in the air we were probably running out of our front doors. And of course we used to get asked all silly questions running round to the fire station. 'Where's the fire?' You'd say, 'I don't know till we get there.' Funnily enough, I was running round just before I got to the Castle Hotel and a piece of the maroon came down and hit me on the shoulders.

The effect of the maroon was very, very good but it had disadvantages, when you had very rough weather. Another advantage was that if like some of the chaps working out at Little Common or something like that and you wasn't quite sure, you could look out and see a puff of smoke that was left in the sky. And, of course at night time you had a terrific flash as well. When, for instance, you're singing your head off in St Andrew's choir and you see an enormous flash go across the church windows, then you knew what it was. You just gently walked out and took off your cassock and surplice and dashed off to the station. But it was very effective and very loud. In fact at one very dry period we had so many fires, that we got down to one maroon and we had to borrow lifeboat maroons off of Hastings to tide us over until the extra supply came in. They were very frightening to a lot of the elderly people in the town when they went off, 'cos it was a terrific bang. If we were in the pictures, the Playhouse or one of those picture houses, the operators there had a little slide all ready. They just pushed it into the slide and it said 'Fire Call' and if we hadn't heard it it was an indication to us there we were wanted.

We were supposed to cover the whole of Bexhill which is, you know, quite a considerable area from Middle Bridge out to Glyne Gap, out to Lunsford Cross. But this was the difficulty in those days because there were so few brigades and there was no co-ordination between the fire service. A lot of brigades would not let their fire service go outside their borough. For instance I well remember when Rye bought a new fire engine. My wife's boss, Freddy Thompson, who owned Thompson and Jewhurst in Town Hall Square, the bakers, he was at that time a town councillor at Rye. When Rye bought that fire engine, they said, 'This doesn't go outside of Rye.' You know it was paid for by the people of Rye and one had to be very careful really because of the back-up.

The same thing applied when we went to Battle Abbey and we took Lady Kitty which was not very old in those days and, of course, she was the only big escape machine that we got in Bexhill. And the Chief, Jim Stevens at the time, had to make up his mind whether he could go. But he said, 'Right, we will go but I'll take a crew of six with me. Now we were a little longer turning out that morning because he said 'Right I'm going to take so and so and so and so, hop on.' Off they went, knowing full well that the rest of us was just left to look after Bexhill. It did make a lot of difference. I can always remember Cyril Smith saying that it was 85 miles on the speedometer and they did the journey in 15 minutes, which is pretty good. As soon as they got up to the top of Sidley they could see the glow in the sky.

Hastings, for instance, they didn't mind where they went. If they got a call to Sedlescombe they would go. But Hastings was not a retained brigade. Hastings were a volunteer brigade. Then later on you had like Brighton was full-time and retained, so many full-time and so many retained men. And at that time a lot of the bigger cities, like Portsmouth and Liverpool, were police fire brigades, run by the police. Hastings, for instance, they had eight stations, four motor stations and four foot stations and they relied entirely on what they got from the insurance companies. They never had any retaining fee. We were retained by the borough council and we were paid five pounds a year retaining fee. Firemen got five shillings for a call. That five shillings had to last for two hours and then you got half-a-crown an hour after that. The year I'm talking about is 1926.

Yes, we were able to do another job. Its only the fact that our employers were so good, and of course even in those days we were well thought of. You know, we were doing a public job. We used to turn out to fires in our best suits and all that kind of thing, and we went straight away.

When the maroon was fired in the day-time there was a shop in Station Road then called Squirrels and they were sanitary engineers and builders. Well the chappie that ran the office there, he had a stop watch 'cos one of his employees, who was my uncle, worked there and he was in a very fortunate position [as] he looked straight up Amherst Road. As soon as he heard the first sounding of the maroon he had his stop-watch ready and when he first saw Percy he started his stop-watch. He then took the time that it took the machine from that time coming down Amherst Road, not waiting on the forecourt, but actually on its way. Its quite true to say that in the hours of daylight the first machine was under way in two minutes.

If we were at work sometimes there were two chaps at Russell's Garage, that was Cyril Smith and Percy Scrace, well they always heard, you know, the first report. They would be coming down London Road by the time the maroon burst in the air. They would run through the short cut where Burstow and Hewitt's Auction Rooms used to be and the Athletic Club, straight into the fire station.

Cyril Smith was so attached to Lady Kitty when it was bought because it was something new. It was the first time that Bexhill had, apart from the old steam fire engine, a pukka new fire engine which in those days was something! It was one of the first fire engines that had four wheel brakes. This was in 1930, one of the first fire engines that ever had a windscreen. It was what was known as a low load

Firemen, Egerton Park, early 1930's. Tom Pratt is on the extreme right and George Pratt fourth from right, both in the back row

machine. It was very easy to get onto. The old ones were very high, what they called the Braber body, you used to have to jump up on one footboard and then up on another one. He, Cyril, was a very keen motor mechanic and also it was the first machine to have a self-starter. But Cyril Smith never used the self-starter. He came to the station every evening and he would start that machine up, and he left it jusf on compression. So he could run in the fire station, he just pulled that handle over and she started straight away.

The Council was very keen to see we had all the best equipment. In those days there weren't many petrol pumps about and that machine was run on Shell Aviation. We had equipment in 1928 down here which was right up to the times, we were very modern, very well equipped.

We had self-contained breathing apparatus, which is something very up to date. They just bought two-cell sets, now the sets just last for half an hour. They were bought from C.B. Gormans, the people who made the Davis Submarine apparatus. This chappie came down and we attended the fire station for three evenings and he put us through the drill of having to put the thing on. You could put that set on by using a piece of poetry. It was kept in a large tin box and you had a dresser, and once you got the tin open it went:

'Whilst the dresser buttons you
Take plug and mouthpiece too,
Main valve open, paper reading,
By-pass, do your breathing.
Nose clip tight, protect your sight,
Thumbs up and you're all right.'

Then you were equipped to go into a smokey atmosphere.

We [got the breathing apparatus] after the gas works fire, you see, which was a big tar tank fire. I wasn't in the brigade then, but that was about 1924. That was the gas works at Ashdown Road. There was a 14 foot tar tank that caught alight. It was in a very dangerous position because right alongside it was tanks of benzine. We were living at Windsor Road and my elder brother was courting at the time and his wife-to-be came from Ninfield, so he was just going out to meet her off the bus. Well he came back and said, 'I'd better get my uniform on, the bang's going up in a minute.' And sure enough it did, and this tar tank burned all the Sunday afternoon. There was a huge pall of black smoke because there was very little foam-making

Before a procession, outside the old station in Amherst Road, circa 1930

equipment then. What they did, as soon as they could get near enough, was they covered all the tanks with sand. They had ample quantities of sand down there. It burned and burned until it snuffed itself out at six o'clock in the evening. It was quite a tricky job.

In the summer months we had quite a lot of self-combustion fires from the hay-stacks. Farming was different in those days. I remember they got called out to Boreham Street, to Redhill Farm, there was a whole stack yard alight; there were cornstacks, haystacks, beanstacks. The farmer used to put them very close together. They got the fire under control but it was going to burn for a long time, as with stack fires they have either got to burn themselves right out or you've got to pull them apart. We used to carry hay knives, brigades do still carry hay knives out in the country today. I remember we had a crew out there for three whole days and nights and we used to change them over at night. It was just a question of damping down and protecting the other buildings.

We were very well equipped in other respects. We were one of the first brigades in Sussex, apart from Brighton, to have what was known as instantaneous couplings. That is you just snapped them together, male and female, and they could be pulled apart with a couple of lugs on the side. We did a lot of competition work in those days. I can well remember that we lent to other brigades, that were competing against us, one or two lengths of hose so they could compete with this instantaneous hose. We always carried two lengths of rubber-lined hose so that if we were going through people's property or through business premises, we could take the rubber-lined hose because with the old canvas hose there was always a certain amount of seepage. It was very valuable for heath fires and bonfires, it stopped the hose from being burned through.

Tim Burgess is on the photograph. He lives at Sidley with his daughter, he is 87. There's Mark Dennett, an uncle of mine, he was in the South African War, at the relief of Ladysmith. The fire brigade was often a sort of family tradition, same as the lifeboat.

We had no cutting equipment for road accidents because it wasn't necessary, there weren't many cars on the road. People used to help us quite a lot, people would give us a lift if we were coming down Sackville Road or something like that. There were a lot of cycles and in those days, you could leave your cycle up against the kerb. Going to a fire you pinched the first cycle you came across, even a trades-man's bike. And all these bikes would be found in a heap outside the Fire Station. The brigade is different today as there are more hazard-ous cargoes carried on the roads. In my time as a call boy along Windsor Road the number of motor-cars was two at the most. People had motor-bikes and side-cars but there weren't many of those about. If anyone got killed on the road it was a terrible.

On the other hand Bexhill was full of hotels and big boarding schools and we had a tremendous responsibility. We probably didn't realise the responsibility we had, when you take the buildings like the Sackville Hotel and like the Metropole. We never had any turn-table ladders. We had to ride to fires on old machines. It was pretty awful sometimes in bad weather, even out to Little Common, on an open machine especially before the fitted windscreens. Every-body was practically frozen to death before you got there.

We had quite an inflated population, especially in the summer. The Sackville used to be full, the Carlton Hotel, the Normanhurst, all those places. And you had all these big schools like Ancaster,

Normandale, Lake House, Winceby House for the girls and St John's for the boys. St Wilfreds had a big fire. I remember that, as a boy. I went out there on a Saturday afternoon. The disaster was made much worse by the lack of water. Although Hastings came over to help us, it was still impossible due to the lack of water as the mains were not big enough.

Today most machines carry about 400 gallons of water. Lady Kitty was the first machine to carry what we called 'first aid' equipment and that water tank only had 40 gallons of water. If you used that water correctly it is surprising what you can do with it. So directly you arrived at a fire you had to assess whether you could put that fire out with ordinary extinguishers, or the first aid and hose and reel. If not you had to find the nearest hydrant and connect up to that to give you a supply into that tank, or give you a supply through another length of hose. These days if you have an ordinary house fire, and you have two machines on the job with 360 gallons on each, it is not often that you have to open up a hydrant. This is a good thing because on a lot of these old roads in Bexhill you are only on a three or four inch main. When you think of the incrustation the size of the main is probably much smaller than that.

It was this disastrous fire at St Wilfred's School that perked everyone up. So a new nine inch main was laid right down from Ninfield Road in Sidley and it came down London Road, under the railway arch, up Western Road and down Devonshire Road and connected with the other main on the seafront. Another thing they did was to build fire hydrants right on top of that main, whereas with the old system the hydrants were right on the pavements. If one of the hydrants was opened up all the discoloured water was pulled into the main so people, over a very wide area, got very discoloured water until it had flushed itself right through.

The fire at Beach Haven was a very interesting fire for me. That fire occurred at six o'clock in the morning. I know, I was just getting up because I was working out at Northiam. It was dead on six o'clock and the caretaker had the option of ringing the bells or firing the maroon and, being a stickler for the rules, he fired the maroon. I was looking out of my window in Reginald Road and I could see this pall of smoke going right along the sea front. I was on the first machine and went up Station Road, turned round into Sea Road by the station and from there we could see the flames coming out of the first floor windows and curling up into the second. It was really going well and we thought we had a rescue job on. But when we got down there we were told everyone was out. There were people there in their nightdresses and with all their bits and pieces. We contained that fire with our own brigade. We were fortunate in one respect as they had taken over additional property up Sea Road, and they had just knocked an opening through the extension because they were all built on the same level. So we were able to direct jets of water to prevent the fire spreading up Sea Road. When you can't save the building on fire then you have got to protect the other property.

We had a lot of fires on the railway with all the steam trains. In those days the railway companies used to clear a lot of that [grass verges at the sides of railways] themselves. We got more fires afterwards, when they didn't clear it after they did away with horses, because the railway companies used to use all that hay to feed their own horses. Where Sainsbury's now stands that was all the stables for railway carts and horses where they had their own depot and their own haystacks. After they became more motorised the railway companies were not so interested in clearing the embankments. The fires weren't only caused by steam trains but also by passengers throwing their cigarette ends out. After electrification fires were dangerous because they burned through the cables. When I was up in Surrey one such fire cut the railway service between London and Portsmouth for many hours as it was the main cable, taking the current right through to the Portsmouth sub-stations.

Another interesting fire was the old farm house at Henley Down that was thatched. We had a very severe winter just before Christmas, it was really bad. When we got out there the ice was so thick and the ground so frozen, we ran the Lady Kitty over two fields at the back as we didn't have portable pumps in those days, and they broke about three inches of ice on the pond to pump water out. Clem Burgess, he's still alive today, he was up on the ladder with a jet into the first floor. With the ferocity of the hose the water was running down his trousers, over his leggings and top boots and dripping off. He'd been up there some time and was due for some relief but he couldn't come down because his boots were absolutely stuck to the ladder. Someone had to go up with an axe to chop the ice away, before he could come down and be relieved up the ladder, the hose was so frozen. I think we finished the job at about six o'clock in the evening, it was a pretty bad day now. We had to have blow lamps to unfreeze the couplings, you couldn't roll the hose. There was a firm in Sidley at that time who were civil engineering contractors, Stephen Careys. They had lorries with gantries on and we had to borrow one of their lorries and the hose was laid on like scaffold poles. We had to cart it back to the station that way. Some of us were unemployed because of the frost and then if you did not work you got no pay. This was in 1932-33.

Battle Abbey was a very bad fire, that was the Abbot's Hall and the Minstrel's Gallery. When Chief Stevens got there, Mrs Du Covey was the Headmistress there, and before she used to keep the school in Hastings Road. She said, 'Stevens, I want you to take charge.' Battle was already there but they'd only got a very small engine. Well they got to work with Lady Kitty on the hydrant outside, and within a very few minutes we'd pumped Battle dry. Fortunately Hastings also arrived so there were three machines there. Somebody said, 'There's a very big lily pond at the back.' So they took Lady Kitty inside and they got to work with four jets from Lady Kitty, and virtually contained the fire before it got to the library. Everybody was hastily engaged in trying to salvage everything from the oak-panelled library, and the whole of the lawns in front of the building were filled up with books and tapestries and paintings. The estimated damage at that time was £100,000, that was a lot of money in those days. For many years many chaps in the brigade had pieces of the molten metal. When the fire was burning it illuminated the stained glass windows as the firemen were working outside. All of a sudden all this lot went 'Whoosh!' and it dropped. There was a lot of silver in the lead then and it was very thick lead. There were lots of lumps of molten lead with lumps of glass and burnt timber. Many had pieces of that. The cause was never known. It was pretty tragic really. It was a very nasty job.

Fires in these big country houses were pretty prevalent in those days and it was nothing to pick up an evening paper and see that so-and-so's mansion had been burnt down. Although people took more care there was more danger in those days. When you think that people had oil lamps and candles. We had no electricity, we went to bed with a candle. I can remember my grandmother, round in Reginald Place, she was cooking by paraffin oil stoves, there was all that kind of thing about in those days, and its marvellous to me that there weren't more fatalities.

To reach the people on the top storey we used the extending ladder and we also had hook ladders, they would use today. They weighed about 14 pounds, they were very light, they had a steel barbed hook. You had a belt with a snaffle, so if there was a tall building, you had to smash your way from one floor to another, so a man would smash a window and take a ladder up on his shoulder, and you had a bobbing line on your back, dropped the line and pulled up whatever you wanted, hose or whatever. It was precarious.

Another thing that was well to the fore in the late 20s and 30s, especially in the hotels and schools, especially after St Wilfred's fire (naturally headteachers got worried about all the girls and boys) so they developed the Davey Automatic Lifeline. They were something about the size of a big alarm clock, we carried two on the machine. A lot of schools had these attached in the dormitories. It was bolted into the wall and it lowered a person at the rate of five feet per second. But people had to be instructed how to use them, you could not use them in a panic. There were fatalities because people did panic. You placed the sling under your arms and just pulled it tight, you got out of the window and as you lowered the next sleeve came up for the next person. But we also had a steel rod attached to a wheeled escape, and if you placed that above a window we could run a line up and over, and we had special sleeves made. That was an idea from the Brighton brigade.

Brighton and Bexhill brigades were very closely knit, and Brighton was the only full-time brigade on the whole of the Sussex coast at that time. We took up all their drills, and they showed us what equipment to get and how to use it. We used to go over there on brigade trips and see them at drill, and we could see the whole thing at work. All you had to have was one man on this line and you could lower these people down as fast as you liked. You could lower a lot of people down in a short time. Occasionally there was an outside staircase. There were not the fire regulations in those days as there are today. I feel very happy that I was in a brigade that was always up to modern standards. A pal brought the chief of Bromley fire brigade down to Bexhill fire station, and I showed him round and he was absolutely astounded at the equipment that we had got. Other places were not so fortunate as many of the retained brigades throughout the country relied on the works brigades to help. Like Guildford, for instance, relied on Dennis Brothers works brigade. If Guildford wanted any help any time they used to get Dennis Brothers brigade to help them.

Eastbourne never had a turn-table ladder until about 1932. You think of some of our hotels and some of Eastbourne's hotels, they are the same sort. Hastings was worse off than we were as I don't think they had a 60 foot escape ladder, which we had. It was originally kept in Devonshire Square, where the taxi rank now is. Then, when Lady Kitty came along, it could be transported. But before Lady kitty, if there was a fire in one of the hotels, four men were regularly detailed to go and get the 60 foot ladder from Devonshire Square, and wheel it down on to the sea front.

'Helena', named after Mrs Russell, was built on an old Johnson chassis. The first one he built was 'Diana' christened by Lady Kitty's mother [Countess De La Warr], which was built on an old Leyland chassis and a Dennis pump fitted up, but it was a Bexhill concoction. Russell also built two ambulances, they were very good ambulances. A lot of the methods he designed are incorporated in the ambulances of today. I remember that when the 'Queen Mary' used to go off on these trips, a very rich lady out Cooden way always used to hire a Bexhill ambulance to take her down to Southhampton. When I went up to Bromley you were not only a fireman but an ambulanceman as well, we ran the ambulances. We used to have to go out to all the accidents in Bromley, we only had two ambulances. It cost you seven shillings and sixpence to go from your house to the local hospital by ambulance, and it was one pound up to a London hospital.

The old steam fire engine was for many years out at Battle, after it left Bexhill Corporation, for which it did a lot of work.

After I left Bexhill the advancement started. In 1938 when I was up at Epsom, they were starting, like all other fire brigades, to train the auxiliary fire service. The government was taking the lead in this, and was supplying money to councils to take on extra firemen to be responsible for all auxiliary fire service equipment that was issued in preparation for the War. I think there were two in Bexhill, one in Sidley and one in Little Common.

All these chappies had to be trained. We used to train them at Bexhill because of the competition work. We never got paid for drills. Drill night was always Tuesday at seven o'clock, and we probably trained on until half past eight or nine o'clock. In the summer when we were practicing for competitions, which we were pretty renowned for in Bexhill, we used to do two escape drills from the escape tower at the back of the fire station. Before that was built we used to use old Sargeant's place in Town Hall Square because that was a suitable place, as it had a flat roof for carrying someone down.

And whilst these two crews were competing against each other, another crew was sent down to the sea front to the Polegrove to get ready for the Coastguard competition, then we had to follow down on the motor pump. We had already had two escape drills and when we got to the Polegrove there would be two teams competing against each other for the Hose Cup. Then there would be two motor pump competitions. Then all that stuff had to be packed and cleaned up and returned to the station. We had to do that twice a week in the spring and early summer ready for the competitions. We did have two of the national camps in Bexhill.

We were in the south coast district, and if you won your district competition, then you would be eligible for competing in the nationals. In the national competition in 1930 there were 300 firemen under canvas on the Polegrove which was used for a whole week for these competitions. I always remember one of the headlines in one of the daily papers, I don't know whether it was the *Daily Mail* or not, said 'Bungalow Fire at Little Common, 300 firemen sleep while bungalow blazes.'

The drill tower was built for practice and drying hoses, the slats on the side allowed plenty of air currents round to dry the hoses. We were not over blessed with hoses, and one had to make sure that as soon as they were dry two or three of us went and got them down so that if they were wanted they were available. I think a 50 foot length of hose in those days cost about five pounds.

We did have a fire alarm system down on the Metropole Hotel. It was a rather primitive affair because all these bell systems were run off what was known in those days as porous pots, enormous things, like big jam jars. They were filled with sulphuric acid and I forget what was the other stuff they put inside, and that formed the basis of the electric current.

154

NELLIE SINDEN

*Nellie Sinden was born 12th July 1912 in her grandmother's home, 1
Sadlers Well Cottage, Hooe. She moved to Bexhill when 14 days old.
This account contrasts the remembered delights of her childhood,
including a wonderful Christmas, with the drudgery and immensely
hard work of being a domestic servant.*

I went to school at the age of five. One wore boots which was the
dress of the day and we more or less wore dark dresses. Everyone
wore dark clothes, black stockings, long coats, and in the winter we
wore fur hats and we had muffs; we never had gloves or mittens, we
had muffs and a very posh blue one that was kept on purpose for
Sundays. We had pinnafores from that age up. If we went to school
and we hadn't got our pinnyfore we were sent home for it. We had
to line up, after the register was called, in front of the teacher to have
inspection for our shoes, back and front, and if she thought they
weren't clean, we were sent home to clean our shoes. Everyone that
went to school wore boots. Lace-ups through the weekdays and
button-ups on Sundays.

I walked to school and was very fortunate because I was just five
minutes away from school, which in another sense made it difficult
if I wanted to play up and not get home, because my mother'd say
'You'll be home by five minutes past 12'. The others that lived further
away were more fortunate in a sense because it'd take them longer
to get home. If I wasn't there then my mother'd know I'd been
playing up. Then when you got home, you just had to take your
things off, wash you hands, lay the dinner table and as you got older
you had to help your mother dish the dinner up.

We had to work, had to do our bit. We helped one another,
everybody helped one another in those days, everybody was very
friendly, everybody knew one another simply because it was a small
community. If your parents were not well, the next door neighbour
would come in and the older ones would help the younger ones to
get ready for school and you'd have to get their breakfast. You'd
have to take them and you also had to bring them home. And then
if you were old enough, you had them to bath and get to bed and you
really had to see to them. So the older ones, where there was a big

family, really were the drudge to the family because the older ones were expected to help mother all she or he possibly could.

Every family had their own allotments. They grew all their veg on it: enough potatoes to store for the winter to help though 'til potatoes came again. That was the late crop, stored in very large wooden tubs which stood on bricks to keep them off the concrete floor (it was concrete so the damp wouldn't come through) covered over with a couple of sacks. The onions were harvested and hung up and done just the same. All you had to buy was fruit and bread unless you ran out and your mother thought she would make it, although the baker used to come round every day. In those days it was delivery by horse and cart.

If we wanted some milk before our own milkman came, there was always a Mr Thomas that come up the road. Us kids used to take our milk-jugs out and he'd line us all up in order and then we'd get our pint of milk which was dished up with a little measure, a pint measure or a half-a-pint which was always hanging on the can. They carried churns on their carts to fill up their cans again. The milkman called twice a day, and in between that they used to come round selling the skim-milk, penny a pint. That made your milk puddings with a knob of butter and a little bit of nutmeg.

If you wanted pickles for dinner which, more or less on Mondays, was always cold with jacket potatoes, you just had to take your pudding basin down to the shop, where they weighed your pudding basin and get a penn'orth of piccalilli pickles and nip off home with it for your dinner. If you were having treacle, you'd have a plain boiled pudding, suet pudding, then you took your basin down and you had a pennyworth of treacle. That was lovely thick rich reddy-brown treacle. After a time everything was done up in tins and bottles and to us, after having that sort of way of living all those years, there didn't seem the taste to it.

As children, when one came home from school, if it was in the winter, we wasn't allowed out. We had to take our school clothes off and put our old glad-rags on. By the time we got home, it was more or less tea-time and we had our tea and there was no electricity or anything, so we had an oil lamp which stood on the centre of the table in the kitchen and we just sat round and read and played games.

We all went to church on Sundays. Sunday School in the afternoon and in the evening. You just went with your parents to church. We never even thought that no we wouldn't go or we didn't want to go.

In the holidays, when I was at school, we had to work all the week doing household chores and we got a penny at the end of the week. But of course a penny went a long way. You could get twenty aniseed balls for a penny and so we used to buy a farthing's worth of sweets at a time.

We got what we could get most of for our money. Popcorns were favourites in those days. You had a packet of white ones done up in a cornet-shaped screw and they weren't sweet but the pink ones were. You were allowed to go down the shop just before you had your bath and buy a packet of white and a packet of pink popcorns. Then you got back and you started to eat the white ones to get rid of them first 'cos they weren't sweet, 'til your bathwater was ready.

No houses had bathrooms and in the winter us kiddies would bath in front of the kitchen fire in the ordinary zinc bath. In those days every girl had long hair. When that was washed, there were some tears shed when that was brushed and combed with all the knots. Every Saturday evening that was done up in tiny little plaits and the ends rolled up in rags. That was all undone before you went to Sunday School and all brushed and combed, then you had this enormous bow on your hair. That was the only time you were allowed to have your hair loose. Going to school you either had one plait or two plaits and you had brown hair ribbon on the end of it. At times the boys at school were rascals and they used to get the scissors and snip a little bit off the girls' plaits in front of them. Just for devilment.

We had our two weeks [school holiday] at Easter, a week at Whitsun and five weeks in the summer. In the summer it was different. They were cutting the hay up in the hay field which was three minutes walk from where I lived. We used to go up there and have a rare old time. Turn it all over, make a hay house and then ask our mothers if we could take our tea up there. We'd make a bedroom and a sitting room and a kitchen and invite the other families.

At the back of our row of houses, there was a track which went down to all the back ways, with a high hedge all the way down and the ivy grew that had the white flowers on it. We used to play mothers and fathers, put long skirts on and old blouses and get this white columbine and twist it round our hair and round our waist and really go to town and decorate ourselves up, decorate our dolls and we paraded up and down the back and no one could see us but we was happy.

Another thing our parents did for us - propped the gate open, it was a wooden gate. They'd tie a good thick rope on the gate post and make a swing for us. Our mothers used to turn the rope and used to skip in along with us. Our mothers joined in our games like that with us.

Hops were growing quite near at Hooe and at Ninfield but I never went. My mother used to go. I was at school. My mother used to stay with my grandmother for the day, and then she had to walk home at the end of the day with a basketful of blackberries and laden with hops. They hung [the hops] round the pictures 'till hops came again. The mothers helped at harvest time. That brought them in that much extra to help them towards winter clothes.

No one ever went away. 24 May was Empire Day when we did have an Empire. Then we never went to school for lessons. But we all got to school at 9.30. All the girls and boys were all in white and we had a red, white and blue rosette pinned on us. We had a hymn and a prayer, and then each class walked behind our teacher, two-by-two, to Egerton Park. All the schools done the same thing and we all met in Egerton Park round the flag-pole. There was a parson there who gave just a very short sermon. We had a hymn and a prayer and then we all sang 'Land of our birth we pledge to thee.' We all walked round the flag, saluted at a certain spot, went back to school and dispersed. In the afternoon, we got back to school at three o'clock, we were entertained by a Punch and Judy show. We were given a bag which contained buns and sandwiches and an apple and an orange and a few sweets. That day was very important to us all. The private schools didn't go down to Egerton Park naturally. Just the elementary schools.

Where the Library is was St Barnabas Girls' School. From St Barnabas School, underneath the arch, right round to the Castle was the barrow boys. No one went to the shop to buy their fruit because there was not that amount of shops in Bexhill. All the barrows had their own lanterns because there was no electricity. The street lamps went by gas and us children used to wait for the lamplighter to come round every evening at five o'clock. He used to pull the chain down

Bexhill school celebration, probably Empire Day, date unknown

with a long rod and on went the light. We used to follow him round for two streets and then indoors quick to get our tea. Sharp at 10 o'clock he would come round and put out the street lights, so the street lights really were only on for about five hours every evening. What shops there were had very large lights with a very large black shade over the top to throw the light down, because there again that was only gas.

The shops shut at eight o'clock. And on a Saturday evening they were open 'til ten. You see the housewife never got her week's wages until her husband came home with the money at five o'clock on a Saturday. When we had our tea and then if the parents wanted anything, you got Saturday evening right round to 10 o'clock to go over the town and do your shopping.

Christmas Eve was a real do for everybody. We got our wages just like at the end of the normal week. The shops closed at 10 o'clock, half-past ten by the time they got the turkeys done. We used to have our tea and our mother banked the fire up with coal and coal dust, shut the little door, put the shovel in front so nothing fell out. And it was bitter! Just like it was in Dickens' times and we had our muffs and our fur hats on and an enormous scarf. We used to set out round the shops to buy all the fruit and nuts off the barrow boys and look at all the Christmas decorations in the shops. In one shop would be Goldilocks; in another one it would be Robin Hood and in another one it would be The Three Bears. In one there was always this train which amused us how it zig-zagged all round on its rails - underneath the different arches and come out. That used to thrill us to bits. And clockwork toys in various shops.

Underneath Sackville Arch, was a couple of barrows. They both had a fire on them. One used to roast chestnuts and the other one did roast potatoes. Us kids had a pennyworth of roast chestnuts done up in a screw of paper, holding them in our mugs. Our parents had jacket potatoes. The man would split it open through the centre, put your salt in and say 'There you are mum! Tuppence.' That kept us warm, and we nibbled them as we walked round the town looking at all the shops that were dressed up and all the paper-chains. There were masses and masses of Japanese lanterns and everyone had candles in and they were all lit. We even had them in our own home. No paper chains were ever bought. Only the coloured strips to make them. And we never made those 'til about just a day before Christmas Eve.

We had Christmas trees and we took our stocking with us and that was tied on the end of the bed. We were so excited but we're told that if we didn't get to sleep Father Christmas wouldn't come, but we used to wake up in the night and grope at the foot of the bed to see if Father Christmas had been. And thrilled to bits because our stocking was filled. 'Mum! Mum! Light the candle quick! Want to see what Father Christmas has left me!' There was always an orange stuffed in the toe and then an apple and then a few nuts, a sugar mouse, a chocolate mouse. A little teddy bear used to sit at the top, a little tiny bag of sweets and there was all these little fancy beads. And you could buy the little old fashioned wrist watch on a strap.

The clock part was made with all little beads. The stocking was packed the same way every year.

When I was in service I had to work [at Christmas]. We didn't finish until five o'clock. The boss gave us presents. And their relatives came and they all gave us a present. I remember the son every year dressing up as Father Christmas, coming in with this enormous hamper full of presents. They were good presents. I'd a wrist watch and I had an umbrella once and I had a blouse and various pieces.

There was a lot of drinking in the town. Some of the husbands were quite rough. Very rough. The police in those days used to go on their beat and do every street three times a day. In the evening between half-past ten and eleven o'clock they would walk all round the streets again and try your front door. And if the front door opened, you were called out 'Hi! You gone to bed up there? Do you know your front door isn't locked?' 'Oh sorry about that!.' 'Well you better come and lock it then.' And the policeman would wait and make sure that your father or your mother came downstairs and locked that front door.

I was eight and a half when my father died. In that day and age it was known as widow's weeds. Everybody that was widowed stayed in mourning for a whole year and they never dreamt of coming out of it afore that year was up. Well if it was in the winter naturally they'd have their winter hat and coat but this widow's weed went completely over the hat and over the shoulders and right down like a very large veil. It could be plain, could be patterned and it could have lace edging all the way round it.

There was only ten shillings for the widow's pension, that was all. I know rent was cheap. Our house was eight shillings a week, so there was two shillings left out of that. So it meant my mother having to go out to work again. She went on at midwifery or helped with an undertaker to do the last offices. As the children got older, naturally they were glad for them to go out and earn what they could to help bring in the money. My mother was clever with her needle so they used to go to jumble sales, buy coats and dresses which were miles too big and take them home, wash them, cut them up, and make coats and dresses for other people's children where there were so many in a family and where she was a widow and help to keep them clothed.

I don't know how my mother started doing midwifery. She went round helping with all these things, sitting up at night like they always used to. So whenever she was wanted the husband (if it was the wife that was ill), the husband would come, or they'd send one of the kiddies along with a note. And she'd sit up during the night and get the kids' breakfast the next morning and do whatever there was. If she was living nearer than the doctor was they'd nip for her first. Then if she thought that was serious enough for the doctor, or she thought she could manage, that would be all right until the doctor could get there.

For the menfolk, there wasn't much work then in Bexhill. Building might have just been starting and those that were lucky to get jobs in Bexhill got them and those that didn't had to go to Battle or Hastings. They had to walk. Bicycles were very, very few and naturally they hadn't the money to afford to buy a bicycle.

Really everybody walked everywhere. If you went to see relations at Ninfield or Hooe or Ashburnham or wherever it was, well you just went on your own two feet. If there were two or three kiddies they were bundled in the pram. Then you had to walk home at the end of the day. Perhaps you had been playing and rushing and tearing about, then you were tired out, but you still got that journey to walk home.

Bexhill was like Sidley and Little Common, a very small community. It was only just beginning to get built up. The town was full of private schools and laundries and it was that which kept Bexhill going, and kept the postman going really and gave employment for more postmen. The postman always did a Sunday morning round delivering letters. Us kids always used to stand out on the front doorstep waiting for the postman to come up the road. In the summer the postman always wore a straw boater which was the shape of a tin bath upside down.

The Downs Laundry - there was a piece of empty ground at the side and they used to put their pegs and their lines up. All the men wore long thick woollen vests with long sleeves which came down to their wrists and pants which came down to their ankles so one could pass by and see a line full of vests, a line full of pants and a line full of men's thick shirts, lines of towels and then on the other side would be lines of ladies' underwear and what have we and pillow cases and sheets.

The pillow cases had to be gophered because there was the frill all round. The same 'as men's shirts. Gophering was just like hair curling really. Two long iron prongs with a long handle like a pair of scissors and you got it hot on the stove. There wasn't gas. You just got it to that temperature and you just carried on gophering and hoping that you wouldn't scorch it and make a hole in it. The stove for the ironers stood in the middle of the room. It was a square stove with four, like four ledges. One side had four ledges and four tiers to it, and four irons on each ledge to each tier which went all the way round. Each ironer had to keep to their two sets of irons. And there was one to do the stoking up to keep the irons going. When it came to stiff collars they were ironed with an ordinary heavy flat iron. The gophering iron was the very small iron, the size of one's hand, flat on top with a little handle but, underneath it was the shape of an egg. As one ironed it so the collar rolled up and took its shape.

On top of all this laundering for the schools and the big houses there was the carpet beating. When they wanted to earn extra money men, used to go round to the schools and the hotels and the private houses with their handcarts, collect the carpets and roll them up, take them down on to the Downs in Little Common Road and beat away to their hearts' content and a long stiff broom to brush it all off; roll it up and take it back and come out with more. That was the only way carpets could be done; there wasn't enough room in the back yard.

There was the business of having the pile upside down. You turned the carpet upside down to role it on the grass for the grass cleaned the pile and brought it up as though it had been shampooed. There was no shampooing done in those days. If you were going to do anything like that you just had to sprinkle it with salt water or tea leaves and go over it with a long handled stiff broom to bring the pile up, and brush it off onto the surround, as it was called, because there was an edging of about four inches left all the way round the room, of lino. Then you had to move all your furniture and pick all that up and then polish the floor all the way round. When one went into service there were no carpet sweepers or anything like that.

After leaving school girls went in a shop. And if there wasn't enough room in a shop it was more or less domestic service and that's all there was. When I first started off work, a friend took me to this job. She saw it advertised in the paper and I started. They took

163

me on a month's trial and I was there nine years - that was my month's trial!

When I started I had eight shillings a week; that was four shillings for my mother and four shillings for me. I had to have 14 morning aprons, seven on and seven off and they were one and eleven pence threefarthings. So it left two shillings and a farthing. And you had to have white caps and afternoon caps and aprons, so really for the first year it took all that you earned to get your rig. When you went into service you wore black stockings, black shoes, long blue overall, white morning aprons and a white cap. In the afternoon you wore a long black dress down to your ankles and a white afternoon lace apron with a little lace cap.

When I was at my first job, I'd been there a year and of course there were six in staff, and I was at the bottom of the ladder. One of the others said to me 'Nellie, the missus wants you.' So I said 'Oh, all right', and that meant you got to quickly put on a clean cap and a clean apron, pull your sleeves down, put your stiff white cuffs on and toddle off to the office, tap on the door and wait for the missus to say 'Come in.' And then she'd say 'Nellie, you've been here a year today.' 'Yes Madam.' 'Well I'm going to give you a rise.' 'Oh thank you madam.' And your heart went up to the heavens because you're going to get a rise. And when she said 'One shilling extra' your heart went down in your boots. So you worked a year to get a shilling rise. And then you said 'Thank you Madam' and you came out, put your other cap and apron on and rolled your sleeves up, took your cuffs off and went on. So that was an extra sixpence a week for you and an extra sixpence a week for your mother.

Then when you'd been a second year, the same thing happened all over again. 'You're going to get another rise' and that was another shilling. So it took two years to get ten shillings.

You got up at six in the morning, left home at half past six, get to work at seven. You finished at nine o'clock at night. By the time you got home it was half past nine, just to say 'Hello mum. How are you? Goodnight!' and up the stairs to bed. That was life.

When you got to work at seven you got your cap and apron on and your old sack apron which we used to wear in those days to keep our white apron clean. Then you started off on your fireplaces. Being the lowest one of the lot, you had the dirty jobs. You had five fireplaces to clean out and do: enamelling the bars, whiten the hearths and then you had 14 steps to do to go down to the cellar every time you wanted your wood and your coal. You got your fire-lighting wood and small coal ready for lighting. You went round with them in your housemaid's box and you did your five fireplaces. After that you'd get the scuttles from each room and go down to the cellar, fill up with assorted coal, give each one a scuttle of coal. Then you'd take the other scuttle and you'd go down to the cellar again and you'd fill up with logs. So every one had its logs.

After you'd done that you had the front steps to sweep down. You had all the brasses on the door which contained a very large knocker, very large letterbox, the keyhole, the handle and a very large bell which you pulled and it ding-donged. Then on the other side of the front door was the handle to be done.

Then you got your little bucket with all your whitening stuff in and you went out and you had six large steps to whiten, one large part to scrub and then you went back in, took that lot in, picked the mat up from the porch. You had that to scrub over and put your mat back. Then you had your hall to sweep through; pick the four mats up and the little mats outside each door. You swept the hall through and polished everything in the hall - the hall stand, the tables, the silver salvers and the brass ones, which the other chambermaid would have ready to pick up the letters on and take the letters round. Then put your mats back. And then it was eight-thirty and you had to lay up the table for everybody. Then you had your breakfast.

After your breakfast you had to carry on with all the washing up and all the cleaning. If anybody rang the bell for more coal, or the chambermaid brought the coal scuttle out, you had to fill it up and she'd carry it back.

You wasn't allowed to touch the letters that came. It wasn't your job. You were at the bottom of the ladder, the skiv in the scullery getting on with all your pots and pans. The amount of brass there was in those days, it took you three hours to get through the brass cleaning and three hours to get through your silver cleaning. The silver cleaning was done once a week.

The sheets went to the laundry, but all the rest were done in the dolly-tub. The bedspreads were done in the dolly-tub. You just went up and down with the old dolly until it was done. There was no spin driers or anything, just a mangle. What went through the mangle you could put through but nothing with buttons or anything. The washing was put out on the line if the weather was all right to get dry. But then again those sort of things were only done when the weather was just right. Then there was all the ironing of them to do.

Spring cleaning was a shocking time. You had six flights of stairs to get to the top floor. There were two single beds in each room; two mattresses on each bed. We had to lug one at a time all the way down, beat and brush it in the garden, carry it up, get the next one and that's how you went on 'til you done all the mattresses.

Then you had all your carpets and your under-felt to roll up, lug that all downstairs and beat that. You were fair whacked before you started paint cleaning. When you finished all your furniture and paint cleaning it all had to be polished from top to the bottom. All we had was ordinary soap - Lifebuoy, Primrose and Sunlight. Primrose soap was about two yards long very nearly. It was floor soap and was cut up in pieces, and put on the shelf to get dry. That was done to economise, to save money. You weren't allowed to touch a fresh bar, you had to use the stale. It was so hard you couldn't get a flipping lather. So what I did, I was a bit crafty at times, I had a little bit of fresh and put a bit of stale back in its place. So I could get a lather. That was common to all the apartment houses, boarding houses, schools, the lot! It was all this hard soap, everywhere, so that you didn't use it up too quick.

Then you had to help dish up the lunch, do all the pots and pans. The scullery floor had to be scrubbed over, the lino, the whitening all the way round. There was a huge copper in the corner where you did your boiling. That had to be whitened and then you carried on, right through 'til you got the evening meal at the end of the day and at nine o'clock you could say you'd finished.

So it was all getting up at six, going to bed at half-past nine or just soon after, and that was your day, day-in, day-out. Saturday as well of course. And Sunday. You only had a Sunday afternoon once a fortnight. You had to share that.

On Sunday afternoon I'd just go home and have a wash and change. And then have a little sit down. Then it was tea-time and then church in the evening. The tea wasn't anything special on Sunday. Just the ordinary baking of cakes and tarts and bread and butter - paste sandwiches. We looked forward to Sunday afternoon. And another thing was, if we could get done and get home by half-past two, at that age we still went to Sunday School. I went to Sunday

School up 'till I was 21.

When I got to 16 the missus wasn't well so she had to give up taking in guests which she did. And I had the housekeeping to do and I trembled in my timbers because she said she would give me so much money, which I had to make that last a week. But she would pay the milkman and the baker. I had all the rest to pay out of this certain amount. By that time Sainsbury's had arrived in Devonshire Road, and she went to Sainsbury's shopping. So I used to have to go shopping Friday afternoons, directly after lunch. She'd write the list out and off I went. When I came back I had to go upstairs to the bedroom, show her everything that I'd bought and she'd say 'How much did you pay for the rashers?' And I'd say so-and-so. 'Well you done better than me with the rashers 'cos I can't buy rashers as cheap as that.' So I was thrilled to bits.

At the end I'd risen to the height of housekeeper. Then I did the cooking and looking after them - eight people. There were only four servants in the end, until they gradually dwindled. I was still doing six days a week with a Sunday afternoon off every fortnight and I had a Thursday afternoon then for a half-day. And if I got done by four o'clock, well I was lucky, that was my half-day.

But when I was 17 I then finished at five o'clock in the evenings. When I got home I used to go to the Girl Guides or Rangers', used to help with the Brownie pack, or Prayer Meeting on a Monday evening, Bible reading on a Thursday evening. I didn't take up dancing 'til later years.

We didn't go in for boy friends much. I could've had boyfriends, I fought shy of them. I wasn't keen on being seen out with the fellers and besides I hadn't the time. If one's friends went out with a boy friend, well they courted for five, six and eight years 'cos it took them all that time to save up enough to get their bottom drawer, for the boys didn't earn all that much. But when they courted they had to be in by nine o'clock. It was all school pals marrying school pals. You went with a boy knowing that you're going to marry him in the end. He was your boy and he was yours for keeps sort of thing.

I didn't think of moving somewhere else. I was quite content to stay where I was. I suppose one gets into a rut and one knows one's work and one's just happy to stay. One couldn't rebel, there was nowhere else to go. If you left one job, you could only get a worse job with harder work. And if you went in a hotel the work was harder because you'd be the last of the staff to arrive and therefore naturally you were given the worst and the dirtiest and the roughest of the work. You couldn't better yourself in any possible way.

EVELYN OLDER

Born Evelyn Edith Louise Stanley in 1918, Mrs Older talks of leaving school at 14 to go into service. She eventually became a cook - 'a lovely job' - and then in 1941 was called up to war work in Page's Garage making aircraft parts.

My father came from Mayfield and his father came with him and an aunt and they lived in number 12 Beaconsfield Road. My mother came from London down to Hastings and married my father and moved into Beaconsfield Road. I think my father was trained to be a saddler but I don't know where. It was all horses in those days. There were two blacksmiths in Sidley, one in Terminus Road, one up in Old Town. Johnny Brook lived in a big house on the main road, don't know if he'd been a farmer - sold it to hospital authorities. We used to use the track across the 'hospital' field to get to the Old Town but we weren't allowed to do. It was all fields from where we lived to St Peter's Church. Cows, sheep, lots of greenery round us. Why they called Beaconsfield Road and all round there the Honies, I don't know. You'd have thought it was to do with bees. Our address was Beaconsfield, the Honies, before they put Bexhill, and it applied to St Georges and Springfield.

My father worked for Davises in Sackville Road, it's a shoe menders now, opposite the library. My mother also did sewing, she was a was a skilled dressmaker because she had the training. She went up to London from Hastings, where she was born, and trained at one of those big stores. She spent four years training from when she left school. She lived in, on the premises, I don't know if it was Harrods or where. When you served an apprentice you had to live in. And when the first war broke out nobody had anything made for them and she was thrown out, redundant. She got married in 1917, she was nearly 30. It was quite old for those days, they used to get married younger. I had a sister and a brother. I was the first.

My father died in 1930 (I was 12) and she brought us up. Because we only had twenty one shillings (ten shillings for herself and five shillings for me and three shillings for the other two). And if she hadn't been a dressmaker we wouldn't have been able to stay where we were. She had customers from all over and some from these roads round. Some customers came to our house. There were people who ran schools and that sort of thing. I think the top price was twelve and sixpence for a dress. She used to have to go and interview them, go out and do a first fitting, go out and do a second fitting and then when I got old enough I used to have to take it there - all for twelve shillings and sixpence. Customers only used to come to her if they were near. She did business with the people who owned the schools, two Miss Wilsons and the woman Hamilton [Thrift House is now on this site]. She didn't do childrens' stuff, it was grown ups, you know. Some people used to go abroad in those days and take six or seven dresses with them. She worked late at night, she was always sewing. Did it for years right up to when she died when she was 72 and she was still making things for my kiddies at 70.

My brother has always lived in Bexhill and he worked opposite to Thalia House, in London Road, at the garage from the time he was 14 until he retired at 65, except for the war break. And my sister worked in Devonshire Road, it was Barker's then, now Gamley's. She worked herself up from being shop assistant to learning the library, taking the library and then the war broke out and they moved out, moved them, lock stock and barrel, all the girls, up to Redhill to pack up the NAAFI [Navy, Army and Airforce Institute] stuff. She got married up there and stayed there till she moved back down here two years ago at the end of this year. She'd been here just under a year when her husband died and they'd got settled in a bungalow up at St Stephen's church. 66 he was.

We all went to school in Barrack Road, to start with, but then my brother was separated from us when we got to a certain age and he went round into Chantry which is now a row of new houses. It was a little school run by Mr Bunting who lived in the Old Town, he was head teacher.

The Sunday School for St Stephen's church was on the bottom of the Downs. I thought it was for Hamilton Hall but it was the Sunday School for St Stephen's. You could go from Cranston Avenue, through a kissing gate into a big tunnel that must have gone under the railway and come out at the top of Reginald Road.

If you were clever at school they had to pass an examination to go to what was the secondary school in Turkey Road, now the College. Only a very few passed. If they passed they were allowed some money towards their books and things. There were no opportunities

Beaconsfield Road

for other kinds of work. Nothing at all, not when we were young, it was shops or service, and for the lads errand boy. My brother was apprenticed over the road at the garage [in London Road] and when my mother went with him to get the job because she was a widow and couldn't pay for his training fees he worked for two years on no money at all and he got three shillings on the third year and picked up to five shillings. He had to buy his tools too. That's why I went into service, so I could give Mum some help. When war broke out and he was only 17. 18 he joined up, and then he went into army.

We never had a radio till just before the war my brother went into Searches. Ron Search talked my brother into having a radio for a shilling a week and it was the first radio we had. We were made up with it.

St Peter's school being a church school when you left they talked you into joining a club that was called the Girls Friendly Society and they did try and teach you a bit of dancing. But then I couldn't get away to do it. We were allowed to church on Sunday so we did, to get out for half an hour.

I left at 14 and went into domestic service. Some lady trained me for two and six pence a week which I went from eight till two-thirty for a year. Did she train me? I just worked hard, I should imagine. But I had several jobs like that until I became a cook in 1937 which was the best job I had, really. But I've always worked in Bexhill.

Bexhill was a very divided place. Three-quarters worked as servants, gardeners, boot boys. Boot boys, they used to do coal and logs and they did all the boots. All those types of people [lived] that side of the town, Dorset Road, Cantelupe Road. All those houses were occupied by one family with not less than three servants. That side - that's where all the work was. Then the shops had a little van and a man who went out to get orders and an errand boy so everybody was employed as staff of the shops and all the people in those big houses were waited on hand and foot. Even half a pound of butter used to be taken out to Cooden. It was quite a journey to get to Cooden. If you had time to have a walk but you didn't have time. In Amherst Road they were all private houses. Big houses employed all the people. There were lots of schools, Manor Road, had the Beehive, with a lot in Hastings Road.

In service you only had half a [weekday] day off three-thirty to ten, and every other Sunday. You didn't have much time to explore. You lived in. Well treated? Well, I won't tell you about that. They didn't treat you as a person. That was the trouble, not any of those I worked for till I became a cook. Then she was a nurse, and so she was more on our level wasn't she? If they gave you meals you had to have the leavings from the dining table. And you always got called by your surname. And if she dropped a newspaper she rang a bell for you to pick it up. I used to get three pounds something a month cause I was getting food and board and a lot of aggravation. We accepted it because it was the way of life.

The last people I cooked for used to cater for families there. It was a lovely job. They moved to Exmouth when war broke out and left me high and dry. I could have gone, but I didn't want to leave. Then I worked for the Arundel Hotel, where the Clock Tower is, by the museum. It was a hotel. I had to get up and go there by seven and I left at nine-thirty, that was in 1939. It isn't the Arundel now. When I tell my children they say 'Mum whatever was the matter with you.' But I was glad of that job cause everybody had scarpered at the start of the war. You couldn't live on your parents and not pay for the food. I can't remember what I paid my mother, about five shillings. She owned the house when my father died. She came and lived with me and and she died in 1959.

At the beginning of the second war all of us with the same initial had to go to the Labour Exchange which was a little hut thing up London Road. Mr Bates was in charge and we was interviewed and told, buses, land etc. You see we were all called up in 1941 and we were directed either to go on the land, or the buses. Mr Page asked to make aircraft parts, we could go to him. I saw Mr Page and started the following Monday with two other ladies. We were absolute babes to it all. I've got a picture of the people who worked with me - it is taken outside Morris House at the end of Sackville Road near the Colonnade. It's of all the workers, day and night shifts, and we all worked at Morris House. It was a big garage opened by Amy

The Morris House workforce, circa 1943. Evelyn Older is in the centre of the front row, on the immediate left of Mr Page

Mrs Older (centre) and Mrs Elphick working at Morris House

Johnson and Lord Nuffield [before the war]. Mr Page, that's the gentleman who owned it in the middle of the photo. It's the Honda Garage site, that is being demolished. It's all in tatters now, it would break Mr Page's heart. I don't think he is alive. He had to have all these lathes and we worked there for four years. We made aircraft parts mostly for the Mosquito bomber - which seldom gets mentioned, I might say. We started with three girls and with a few men and it multiplied to 25 people a day and 25 a night, in all just over 50 people. It was a war industry. From the outside you wouldn't have known what we were doing. It looked just like a garage. They did a few repairs.

I know Bexhill Motors in London Road did something too, cause we went on a union do. They didn't do what we did, they did something to do with the caps, metal shells or something. We weren't supposed to talk about it. All the garages were taken by the Ministry and told to do these things but we did aircraft parts. Mr Page made me foreman and the foreman from Bexhill Motors went with me. He made me foreman in the end cause you know what women are, they couldn't bear umpteen women going in, so he said, you're a good talker so you be their spokesman. I was forewoman. Only because he couldn't deal with women, poor man had no experience of dealing with women. I was there four years, August, dead four years to the month. I had had to do it, I was re-directed. You weren't allowed to stay at home and do nothing. So I left in 1945. I'd gone straight from cooking. Mind you, I enjoyed it. It was so interesting, I was turning the lathe, and they gave us some tuition. The boys didn't know much, it was just trial and error, it was sharpening the tools which used to get me.

I got married in 1940, I was 22. My husband was Bexhill born in Chandler Road, I'd known him for three years before I married him, well he went into the the services, that's what hurried it, didn't it? He was only an errand boy, no way we'd have got married on errand boy's money, could we? But then he went into the services and there was a prospect. He was in the desert for five years. He wasn't the only one. We were all in the same boat. He came back and went to Earls the baker. He had started with Hudson's grocers in St Leonards Road, and worked his way up, and when he came back Hudson's had left the town, because they were supposed to take you back, you see, after the war. But there wasn't a job, so he went to Earls for a little while and then he went on to a taxi firm for the rest of his working life.

All the time he was in the services I lived at Beaconsfield Road with my mother. We stayed there and had two little children and eventually they gave us a house in Watermill Close which they had just built. I had got two small children when I moved - I had the oldest one and 13 months later I had another daughter and then a man came to see where I was living and I think he nearly fell over, a double bed, a cot and another bassinet, in front of the window and I think he felt we were slightly overcrowded. So I went up to the new house and stayed there for 38 years and then came down here into a new flat. I haven't done bad have I?

This road where we live now, London Road, was Upper Station Road and Lower Station Road was from the Town Hall to crossroads. Lower Station Road from Belle Hill up till the flats was called North Road. The gap by Sedgewick Road and the top bit was called London Road. We think that's where London Road came from. So London Road was only the bit at the top. We had pigs. It was all farm land round Sidley station. A huge field where hospital is. From where Hospital is, right way down, to the alleyway that goes to Old Town. From St Peters Church right the way down they were all fields with no houses. You could walk through there, horses and things. The Railway kept their horses that pulled the carts and delivered for the station down where the toilets are now in Town Hall Square. They had a big place and you could see the horses. They used to unload the horses where Sainsbury's is. They had a big yard there, station yard, unload them and bring horses down to the stables. There were market stalls further down past Sainsbury's entrance. Horses were near Warburtons, lower down, by the lorry entrance. They had tethers with drink places, fed them and kept them there all night.

I didn't like the beach very much. I can just remember the wreckage round the Glynde Ascent. It was very low and we used to go out there but we didn't realise how deep it was.

I never had a holiday for 40 years after I got married. I never went away. But since 1970 I've done National Tours every year. Two years ago the National gave me a free Christmas. They gave me two T-shirts, travel bag, and then we got flowers at the hotel. This year it's my seventeenth Christmas with National, all over the place, four in Wales, or up in Scotland, five days at Christmas. Isle of Bute one year, Trossachs, Ruthin Castle, Scotland this year, March and April in Scotland, and Scotland again in October then Wales and the Lakes.